Understanding Systems Leadership

Understanding Systems Leadership

Securing Excellence and Equity in Education

Dame Pat Collarbone and
Professor John West-Burnham

network
continuum

Continuum International Publishing Group
Network Continuum
The Tower Building   80 Maiden Lane, Suite 704
11 York Road   New York, NY 10038
SE1 7NX

www.networkcontinuum.co.uk
www.continuumbooks.com

British Library Cataloguing-in-Publication Data
A catalogue record for this book is available from the British Library.

ISBN: 9781855394551 (paperback)

Library of Congress Cataloging-in-Publication Data
A catalog record for this book is available from the Library of Congress.

Typeset by YHT Ltd, London
Printed and bound in Great Britain by Cromwell Press

Contents

Introduction   vii

1 The changing context of educational leadership   1

2 Understanding system leadership   13

3 *Every Child Matters* – cooperation and collaboration   26

4 Leading extended services in an educational setting   37

5 Leadership beyond the school   49

6 Leading networks, clusters and federations   61

7 Educational leadership and the community   71

8 The knowledge, qualities and behaviours of system leaders   82

9 Change – remodelling for personal and organizational change   97

References   109

Index   114

Introduction

The focus of this book is one of the most significant changes ever in the understanding of the nature and purpose of educational leadership in England. For a generation, educational leadership has been understood in terms of institutional leadership: the responsibility for the success and effectiveness of a specific school or college. A primary component of effective leadership was defined as the implementation of national and local education authority policies at school level. A range of forces is now challenging that model; the extent of the change in thinking is perhaps best exemplified by the recent change in title from the Department for Education and Skills to the Department for Children, Schools and Families. This is more than a symbolic or superficial change; it represents the latest stage in a radical rethinking of the education system in England. The most significant examples of this change are to be found in a range of policies, strategies and initiatives:

- the Children Act/establishment of Children and Young People's Services
- School Improvement Partners
- extended services
- *Every Child Matters*
- clusters and federations of schools
- Building Schools for the Future/the primary capital programme
- personalizing learning and the impact of information and communication technology (ICT)
- changes in the 14 to 19 curriculum.

There comes a point when the cumulative impact of innovation within a system can no longer be accommodated by that system in its original guise and the movement is then towards system transformation. This book explores one dimension of that transformation – the implications for existing models of school leadership.

In this book we have tried to bring together, for the first time, all the elements that point to a fundamental reconceptualization of school leadership. This is not to argue for the end of traditional models of headship but rather to identify the components of a far more complex and multi-faceted approach to leadership across the system rather than within the school. As Fullan (2004) puts it:

> A new kind of leadership is necessary for breaking through the status quo. Systematic forces, sometimes called inertia, have the upper hand in preventing system

shifts. Therefore, it will take powerful, proactive forces to change the existing system (to change context). This can be done directly and indirectly through system thinking in action. These new theoreticians are leaders who work intensely in their own schools, or national agencies, and at the same time connect with and participate in the bigger picture. To change organizations and systems will require leaders to get experience in linking to other parts of the system. These leaders in turn must develop other leaders with similar characteristics. (page 9)

This implies a significant realignment of our thinking:

That starts with leadership. We need to develop a new generation of leaders who come to the task with a different understanding of the job and with a different skill set than previously required. Being masters of space and place must yield to proficiency with connection, communication and collaboration. Superintendents of schools must become superintendents of learning. We need to retool our current leaders to remake the system top to bottom. (Houston, 2004, pages 2–3)

We do not underestimate the significance or challenge of these changes, not least in the nature of relationships:

There will always be a tension between local and vertical authority. Systems thinking means that both parties are empowered and move toward mutual influence. In systems thinking, those at both local level and at the centre take into account each other's world, i.e. their world-view enlarges. Recall Senge's phrase – 'a shift in mind from seeing ourselves as separate from the world to connected to the world' . . . (Fullan, 2004, page 12)

The problem is that the process we are describing is not a matter of switching between binary opposites. There is a complex and challenging interregnum between the old and the new – and they will overlap, with inherent contradictions, for years to come. For example, it is already clear that the current models of accountability and inspection do not fully reflect the new reality of *Every Child Matters* and the emergence of Children and Young People's Services. Think of two tectonic plates, grinding against each other, generating heat, creating uncertainty and growing tension until eventually the tension breaks and a new landscape is created. This book offers a model of system leadership that is derived from an analysis of current trends in the English education system – although we recognize that many principles and much practice are still emerging.

We hope that we have contributed to the thinking on the future shape of school leadership, helped to clarify the current situation and supported the growth of understanding so that the debate is better informed.

We are very grateful to Ingrid Bradbury who managed the production of the manuscript with her usual skill, efficiency and charm.

Pat Collarbone
John West-Burnham
November 2007

1 The changing context of educational leadership

Today, many things indicate that we are going through a transitional period, when it seems that something is on the way out and something else is being painfully born. It is as if something were crumbling, decaying and exhausting itself, while something else, still indistinct, were arising from the rubble. (Havel, 1994)

An overview

This chapter is a brief overview of the current agenda facing schools and their leaders as the twenty-first century nears the end of its first decade. It is limited in its analysis and has only briefly mentioned many pressures, including personalized learning, the changing school workforce and the schools' capital programmes. These issues will be dealt with in more depth in other parts of the book.

The main aim of this chapter is to lay out a context to explain why system leadership is an important option both for policy-makers and for school leaders. The remainder of this book looks at this issue in greater detail.

The industrial revolution

The industrial revolution ... enormously increased the capacity of some groups, mostly Europeans at first, to produce goods and services. It greatly altered the distribution of wealth and poverty around the world ... (National Centre for History, cited in Worldmapper, 2007)

At the turn of the final century of the last millennium, the UK was the wealthiest country on Earth, measured by gross domestic product (GDP) per population. At that stage, official figures suggest that GDP per person stood at $4,492. Just over 100 years later, the figure has risen to $25,713 per person but the UK has slipped to twenty-fifth in the table. If we remove countries with populations of less than 10 million, the UK rises to ninth in the table but the number of recognized countries has dropped from 228 to 77. Western Europe still tends to dominate, with four countries above the UK in this second table and 14 countries in the larger table but both Asia and North America have begun to make serious inroads, as has Australia. China and India remain well down the table but their position is rapidly improving. It is likely that the UK will continue to lose its economic position on the world stage, even though individual wealth will continue to rise.

The schools that were built in the latter half of the nineteenth and the first half of the twentieth centuries, at least for the majority of the population, were designed to accommodate children so that they could receive a basic education. The children of working class families in the early nineteenth century received very little education except through the Sunday school system, which grew in popularity until more than 75 per cent of working class children were receiving such an education by the 1850s. The growth in Sunday school education was the direct result of the growing working populations in the expanding cities, which expanded as a result of the industrial revolution and the Church's desire to ensure that working class children received at least a moral education. Over the same period, the number of private schools grew, offering opportunities of a basic education for working class children, but much of this was 'patchy' and often amounted to childcare rather than schooling. However, the growing realization that there were increasing social problems and rising educational aspirations finally led to the government passing legislation in 1870 which provided for free and compulsory elementary education for all children between the ages of 5 and 13. Almost 75 years later, the 1944 Education Act increased the leaving age to 15 and drastically altered the nature of secondary-aged schooling. It would be almost 30 years before further legislation raised the compulsory leaving age to 16, by which time comprehensive schools had replaced or were replacing the grammar and secondary modern schools that originated as a result of the 1944 Act in the majority of local education authorities in England. The compulsory education and training age will rise to 18 by 2015, although this does not mean compulsory schooling.

In many ways, by the 1970s, the class system, prevalent in the UK throughout the industrial revolution, had begun to break down, with many of the country's most creative people proud of their working class roots. Thirty years later it is difficult to argue that there remains a continuing working class, although many would still proudly claim their working class roots, particularly since industrial production in the UK is facing a steep decline.

> An unexpected fall in June's industrial output highlighted the fragility of the recovery in Britain's industrial sector. A decline in energy supply and the output of utility companies caused the drop in production, the Office for National Statistics reported yesterday. (Balakrishnan, 2006)

However, there is a clear rise in a new underclass with the Church of England estimating that 11.4 million people are living below the poverty line with 3.4 million being children.

The knowledge age

Imagine a world where learning happens regardless of location. Where students and teachers connect to each other and the resources they need, simply, quickly and securely. And where education is seductive, engaging and personalized – so that every one of your students has the chance to reach their full potential. (Microsoft, 2007)

In 1969, Peter Drucker, the American management guru, posited that the developed countries were on a course of transition from an economy based on material goods to one based on knowledge (Drucker, 1969). Such an age has the characteristic that knowledge forms a major component of any activity and this is reflected in education, research and development, mass media, information technologies and information services. What Drucker believed was that this would change the nature of economic, social, cultural and all other human activities in existence at the time. Of course knowledge societies are not a new concept. Knowledge has always been what has underpinned the development of the human race and the fundamental additive to the social capital of any human community.

Drucker's and subsequent visions, however, painted a new picture in which it was asserted that we would become dependent on a huge volume of knowledge and information in order to manage our affairs and, of course, awareness of the necessary knowledge would be the key to economic survival. In such an age, the major product for trade and social survival is knowledge.

Throughout our development as a viable species, access to and the availability of knowledge has been not only the key to our existence and survival but also the key to power. One hundred and forty years ago, Karl Marx published *Das Kapital* which was fundamentally founded on knowledge capital. What he could not predict was the development of new technologies, initially in the form of computers.

The invention of the printing press by Johannes Gutenberg in the middle of the fifteenth century was to change access to knowledge for millions but access to the internet, developed throughout the last 20 years, has changed that agenda beyond recognition. With current technologies, we need not be constrained by geographic proximity and it offers many more possibilities for sharing, archiving and retrieving knowledge, as well as allowing ourselves to easily run our own websites and communicate with the rest of the world. In other words, it is now the case that knowledge has become the most important capital in the present age. This means that a focus on knowledge becomes the driver that drives the success of any society, and future success depends on how it is harnessed.

Professor Seymour Papert has argued since the 1960s that the key to learning rests with the technology demands made on a generation of children, now identified as 'Homo Zappiens':

> School is a place where students learn largely by working on projects that come from their own interests – their own visions of a place where they want to be, a thing they want to make or a subject they want to explore. The contribution of technology is that it makes possible projects that are both very difficult and very engaging.
>
> It is a place where teachers do not provide information. The teacher helps the student find information and learn skills – including some that neither knew before. They are always learning together. The teacher brings wisdom, perspective and maturity to the learning. The student brings freshness and enthusiasm. All the time they are all meeting new ideas and building new skills that they need for their projects. Some of what they learn belongs to the disciplines school has always recognized: reading, writing, mathematics, science and history. Some belong to new disciplines or cut across disciplines. Most importantly, students and teachers are learning the art and skill and discipline of pursuing a vision through the frustrating and hard times of struggle and the rewarding times of getting closer to the goal. (Papert and Caperton, 1999, pages 2–3)

A similar view has been expressed for a number of years in England by Professor Stephen Heppell. Heppell now suggests things are changing:

> Of course, back in the last century, schools, teachers and students would have to wait for some central policy directive to guide them: a 'strategy' document, a White Paper, a ministerial speech, an inspection framework. Past guidance included the 'correct' number of keys on a computer keyboard! With mobile phones, they waited for a decade or so for policy to notice handheld technology, whilst a whole generation of children missed out. But the wait is over; schools have decided that anyway, in the 21st century, they should simply get on with it and leave strategy, policy and speeches struggling (and failing) to keep up. As a result schools all over the place are embracing handheld and pocketable technology and doing some very cool and creditable things with it. (Heppell, 2007)

The child in our schools today is perfectly comfortable with technology and sees it as his/her friend. The development of the games console generation means that children are much more astute at multitasking and non-linear problem solving than their parents and grandparents. It is also a generation benefiting from networking and collaboration. The simple fact that many of the pupils in our schools are much more astute with technology than their teachers is already leading to more cooperative teaching and the co-creation of learning which bodes well for the personalization of learning and the development of a more facilitative and coaching role for teachers.

The school for the knowledge age is a very different place than what was required for education in the industrial age and, in England, there is a real chance to recognize this through the *Building Schools for the Future* and the *primary capital* programmes. The country's best architects are working with local authorities and educators to design schools that will need to last at least the next 25 to 30 years and meet the ever changing demands on schools. The academies' programme, from an architectural perspective, is in many cases even more lateral in its thinking. In previous generations, schools were barely open for more than 15 per cent of a student's life. Growing demands for provision mean that, in future, some schools will be open for upwards of 50 per cent of the year with 24/7 virtual provision. This calculation is based on schools being open from 8.00am to 10.00pm, six days a week, most of the year around.

In summary, the key issues are:

1 Personalization is a necessity if schools are to continue to be the key providers of appropriate and relevant learning experiences for children and young people in the future. This is already leading to major curriculum changes and a concerted push on assessment for learning and new approaches to the assessment of learning at national level. Many schools are already beyond this and are developing rapidly.

2 New technologies are not only providing exciting and stimulating opportunities for learning but also are beginning to ensure that appropriate and accurate data are available in order to inform the teacher, the child or young person and their parents. In the past, the lack of such data has left the user in the role of simply another opinionizer, no matter how professional and informed by experience that opinion may have been. Modern teachers have the opportunity of being more unconsciously competent than teachers in previous generations. However, they will need to accept that their pupils are beyond them with an understanding of the technological age and view them as co-creators in the learning process.

3 The capital programmes, currently underway in both the primary and secondary sectors, provide new opportunities to develop the standard learning environment. Mistakes will be made but we need to learn quickly from these mistakes, address them and move on. The exploitation of available resources for children and young people, their parents and the communities they come from has to be a rallying cry to justify the level of investment. There is no longer any justification for a school being available for use in a year, at a level of barely 15 per cent of a student's life in that year.

For the headteacher of a school, each one of these issues will present opportunities and challenges. The headteacher, more than anyone else in the school, has the authority to decide aims, purpose and direction. The journey on which they embark may well decide future outcomes for many of their pupils.

Addressing the issues

When Labour was elected to government, in 1997, it was clear that change was high on the agenda and education was a priority target. In order to drive its vision Labour adopted a command and control agenda and within two years of coming to power there was both a National Literacy and Numeracy Strategy, pushing standards in the primary sector. At first it appeared to be working – and working very effectively, despite complaints and criticisms from the education sector. By the start of Labour's second term in office, in 2001, it appeared that progress might be stalling and the strategies on their own might no longer be enough. A new approach was needed and the government was beginning to suggest that it was ready to trust schools more and see them as the levers of reform.

The groundwork had already been laid with the publication of the Green Paper, *Teachers Meeting the Challenge of Change* (DfEE, 1998). While the technical paper that followed may have been disappointing, there was no doubt that the government viewed leadership, at whatever level, as key to driving the agenda. In the Green Paper, school leaders were promised a national college and were told:

> Good heads are crucial to the success of schools. We need to develop strong leaders, reward them well and give them the freedom to manage, without losing accountability. We want to offer schools freedom to recognise leadership by other teachers who help the head give strategic direction in schools. (page 21)

While the role of headteachers and school leaders has moved on since this, there is no doubt that this Green Paper laid down the leadership challenge.

The publication of the Green Paper *Schools: Building on Success* (DfEE, 2001) provided the first hints of the changing agenda and expectations on schools.

> The reforms since 1997 have been driven from central Government. This was necessary in order to generate a new sense of urgency, to create a new culture focused firmly on standards and to demonstrate that step-change in pupil performance was not only possible but could be achieved rapidly. The creation of the Standards and Effectiveness Unit in the DfEE was an important part of that, as was the continuation and extension of the role of OFSTED. (page 91)
>
> ... At the broader level, it was always the intention, once the culture had begun to change and success was evident across the system, that schools and teachers, at the

frontline, would play an increasing part in reform. In a rapidly changing world, only by encouraging innovation at school level will the education system be able to keep up with other sectors. Moreover, the systematic application of the principle of intervention in inverse proportion to success implies, by definition, that as the system improves Government will need to intervene less. We should increasingly see schools which earn greater autonomy and reward in return for demonstrating good performance. (page 92)

This Green Paper and the subsequent White Paper were mainly addressed to the secondary sector but the primary sector's chance was to come with the publication of *Excellence and Enjoyment: A Strategy for Primary Schools* (DfES, 2003).

In 2004, *A New Relationship with Schools*, the joint publication by the DfES and Ofsted, further enhanced the concept of reform leadership at the frontline and recognition that this required greater interdependency between schools themselves, between schools and their local authorities, and between schools, local authorities and central government:

> In this context the time is right for a new relationship between government and the profession which:
> - builds the capacity of schools to be effective learning institutions with rigorous self-evaluation, strong collaboration and effective planning for improvement
> - delivers an intelligent accountability framework that is rigorous and a lighter touch, giving both schools and parents the information they need
> - makes it easier for schools to access the support they require without duplicative bidding, planning and accountability systems
> - puts in place a simpler, streamlined school improvement process based around a school's own annual cycle of planning, development, reflection and evaluation
> - enables a unified dialogue to take place between schools and the wider education system. (DfES/Ofsted, 2004, page 3)

Throughout this period there has been a number of education acts designed to put the law in place to make this vision a reality. These include Education Acts in 2002 and 2005 and the Education and Inspections Act 2006.

Throughout its second term, the government laid out the groundwork for greater autonomy for schools. But such autonomy requires greater responsibilities and this is just one example why there is now more of a greater need for system leadership from school leaders, on a scale never before required. This does not mean the standards agenda has been quietly forgotten. Rather it is the case that the standards agenda has been re-visioned in order to accommodate the continuously changing agenda.

Improving equity

Since 1997 the government has moved on gender, race and disability issues. It has also heavily funded, through a variety of initiatives, many challenges in schools associated with deprivation using entitlement to free school meals as an indicator. This measure is now being challenged and it has been suggested that prior parental qualification is a better indicator, on the grounds that this may be a better indicator of parental aspirations and therefore young people's aspirations.

According to the DfES (now the Department for Children, Schools and Families (DCSF)) there is evidence of a persistent social class attainment gap at GCSE, although it has narrowed from 29 to 24 percentage points between 1999 and 2003. However, it narrows to a lesser extent if 5+A*-C GCSEs include English and maths.

There are also serious social inclusion issues. One of the more serious is as a direct result of the 9/11 suicide plane bombings in 2001 in the USA and the subsequent 7/7 bombings of the tube in London in 2005. This has raised suspicion of the Muslim community, a long and well-established community in many parts of the UK.

Education, education, education was the rallying cry that brought the Labour Party to power in 1997, with its focus on economic development, equity and social inclusion. This emphasis on education has led to an increase in real term per pupil revenue expenditure of 53.2 per cent between 1997 and 2007. This significant increase in expenditure has brought its own demands.

The 1988 Education Reform Act introduced both the National Curriculum, with its assessment and testing arrangements, and self-managing schools. More public accountability through Ofsted inspections and school performance tables quickly followed in the early 1990s but it was the 1998 Standards and Framework Act that really put the emphasis on standards. This was also the period when the National Literacy and Numeracy Strategies were first introduced in the primary sector. The standards agenda is now a lot more sophisticated with an Early Years Framework, a primary strategy, a Key Stage 3 strategy and a 14 to 19 Framework, all with an emphasis on raising standards (DCSF, 2007a).

There is a lot of evidence to suggest that the government's focus on standards has indeed raised outcomes in literacy, maths, science, and at GCSE and A level. There is also evidence to suggest that background, for example gender, deprivation or ethnicity, continue to make a real difference in attempting to improve pupil performance and, in particular, close the 'attainment gap'. It is true, however, that some progress has been made over the past ten years.

The Millennium Cohort Study, being carried out by the Centre for Longitudinal Studies (2007) at the Institute of Education, which is tracking 15,500 'children of the new Century' born in the UK between 2000 and 2002, has generated a large range of findings on children's upbringing, family backgrounds and development.

The Centre's findings (to date) show (among other things):

- Many children from disadvantaged backgrounds are up to a year behind more privileged youngsters educationally, from as early as the age of three.
- Almost three-quarters of the children with single parents have been growing up in poverty. The proportion of Pakistani and Bangladeshi children in the survey living below the poverty line is almost as high.
- Nearly one in four three year olds is overweight or obese.

The government has continued to attempt to address these issues through a range of initiatives. Here are just some of the examples of initiatives the government has introduced since 1997 to address equity and social inclusion issues, and close the attainment gap between the most and least well-off. There have been initiatives, such as Excellence in Cities (EiC) and Excellence Clusters programmes, with beacon schools, EiC action zones and City Learning Centres, and there has been a strengthening of the specialist schools agenda, such that over 80 per cent of secondary and several special schools are now specialist, and, in the early 2000s, there was the Leadership Incentive Grant. Perhaps more controversially has been the introduction of the Academies, which are a state funded secondary schools programme, a version of the Conservatives' controversial City Technology College programme, and more recently the concept of trust schools.

However, the most radical aspect of the government's agenda for the future of public services and their impact on children and young people occurred in 2003 with the publication of the Green Paper *Every Child Matters* (HM Treasury, 2003).

Every Child Matters

The *Every Child Matters* agenda sets out a long-term vision and entitlement for every child and young person:

- **Being healthy:** enjoying good physical and mental health and living a healthy lifestyle.
- **Staying safe:** being protected from harm and neglect and growing up able to look after themselves.
- **Enjoying and achieving:** getting the most out of life and developing broad skills for adulthood.
- **Making a positive contribution:** to the community and to society and not engaging in anti-social or offending behaviour.

- **Economic well-being:** overcoming socio-economic disadvantages to achieve their full potential in life.

While it may initially have been felt by schools that they were already contributing to this agenda and that they could be left to get on with things, this was to change in 2005 with the introduction of extended schools. There had been an earlier attempt to promote this concept through Full Service Extended Schools (FSESs): at least one exists in the most deprived area of every local authority area. However, they are limited in the number of children and young people who can access the services provided. The government realized it needed a simplified but more expansive programme if it was to have the desired impact.

In June 2005, the then Secretary of State for Education and Skills, Ruth Kelly, announced a new entitlement for every child and young person, their parents and their communities:

> Schools are at the heart of our communities and it makes sense to extend the services they offer beyond the traditional school day. By 2010 all children under 14 who want to, could have access to breakfast and after-school clubs offering exciting activities from 8am to 6pm. These would give them the opportunity to keep fit and healthy, to acquire new skills, to build on what they learn during the school day as well as have fun.
>
> I want parents to shape how extended services develop in their child's school and I want schools to ask for their ideas. We're not expecting teachers to deliver these services but for schools to work with providers in the voluntary and private sectors, support staff and other children's services to develop their local provision. (DfES, 2005b)

The actual offer is more extensive than set out in the above quote and includes:

- Primary schools provide access to **high-quality childcare**, 8.00am–6.00pm, five days a week, 48 weeks a year, in accordance with their communities' needs, combined with **a varied menu of activities (study support)** to enhance achievement and broaden interests.
- Secondary schools provide access to **a varied menu of study support and enrichment activities** that provide fun and stimulating activities for young people, as well as a safe place to be.
- Schools provide access to **parenting support**, including information sessions for parents of pupils joining Reception and on transfer to secondary school; signposting to national and local sources of information, advice and support; access to parenting groups using structured, evidence-based parenting programmes; and family learning sessions to allow children to learn with their parents, where consultation has shown there is a demand.
- Schools ensure that children with additional needs are identified as early as possible, are provided

with **swift and easy access**, and are well supported through integrated working with other services. This means working more closely with the necessary services in the public sector and the voluntary and community sector.

- Schools ensure they provide **community access** to appropriate facilities, such as ICT suites, sports and arts facilities, and also provide access to adult learning.

Many schools may choose to develop an even richer mix of services and activities; this is a matter for them and the communities they serve to decide. To date, over 40 per cent of the 22,500 schools in England are providing access to this offer and the majority of the others are providing aspects of it.

There has been criticism that such an extensive commitment to out of hours working and providing access to a wide range of services may lead to many schools becoming sidetracked and losing their focus on raising standards and pupil achievement, but the Department's response has been to suggest that there are 'no school standards without *Every Child Matters* [ECM] and no ECM without school standards'.

The implications for school leaders

In January 2007, PricewaterhouseCoopers published an independent study into the state of school leadership in England for the DfES. It identified five broad models of school leadership in existence:

> **Traditional model** – the leadership team is comprised exclusively of qualified teaching staff and typically includes a headteacher supported by deputy and/or assistant heads
>
> **Managed model** – this model moves away from the traditional model towards a flatter management-style structure in which specific roles are allocated on the senior leadership team for senior support staff
>
> **Multi-agency managed model** – this model is a natural progression from the managed model and is, in a sense, borne out of the imperatives of the ECM and 14–19 agendas. Like the managed model it involves a flatter, management-style structure, but is more outward looking and inter-agency focused
>
> **Federated model** – this model is characterised by varying degrees of collaboration between schools and sometimes between schools and other providers, for example: 'whole town' approaches to schooling; shared strategic governing bodies, with

executive heads overseeing several schools; and federations between schools, Further Education and work-based learning providers

System leadership model – this model embraces all the different roles that heads can assume beyond the boundaries of their own school i.e. those that contribute to the wider educational system at a local, regional or national level. (adapted from PricewaterhouseCoopers, 2007, pages ix–x)

The fulcrum and lever necessary to accommodate these changing roles is the cultural shift in thinking created by the knowledge age. It was Albert Einstein who suggested that we cannot solve problems by using the same kind of thinking we used when we created them.

It is the aim of this book to explain what we mean by system leadership and why we believe it is a necessary, although not sufficient, condition for school leaders of the future if schools themselves are to have any further relevance in our society. Teachers are no longer, if ever they were, the gatekeepers of knowledge. Schools are no longer, if they ever were, the guardians of a child's acquisition of learning. If schools are to continue to make a positive and necessary contribution to society, if we are to continue to justify the growing cost to the taxpayer and, most importantly, if we are to continue to appear relevant to the needs and aspirations of Homo Zappiens then it is essential that we take on the challenge presented by an agenda focused on schools leading reform. One way that this can be achieved, we suggest in this book, is through system leadership. What we mean by system leadership is defined in the next chapter.

2 Understanding system leadership

System leadership is a potentially ambiguous term as it has very different connotations according to context. It is probably best known in the context of systems thinking as developed by Peter Senge (1990). This approach has been highly influential as an academic theory, and as a proven strategy for enabling organizational development and change. In particular, the theory of the learning organization has led to a rethink of many of the fundamental principles of organization theory. Although there are many interpretations of systems theory, certain features predominate:

- A system has to be understood as a set of relationships in which the whole is more than the sum of its parts and the system has to be viewed in terms of the interactions between its constituent elements.

- Systems work in a highly interdependent manner; a change in one element is likely to lead to changes in others.

- Because of their complexity, systems are best managed by those in direct contact with them rather than those operating at a higher level.

- Systems are often best understood as coalitions of multiple perceptions; there is no objectivity but rather competing versions of reality.

- Change in systems is therefore a matter of relearning realities, of re-educating and so changing perceptions.

Even the most cursory reading of these criteria will confirm that schools are systems within systems and there is much to be learned from systems theory in its formal, academic, sense:

> If you're a systems thinker in school planning, then you focus not on particular practices but on building collaborative relationships and structures for change. You

need mechanisms and a process that allow people to talk, across grade levels, departments, and schools within a system. (Senge et al., 2000, page 394)

In many ways, the reforms that were identified in Chapter 1 are an implicit recognition of the points made above. System leadership in education is all about interdependency, new relationships and ways of working. Schools are very much more than the sum of their parts, as is the education system as a whole. The implications of these arguments and those presented in Chapter 1 have been increasingly recognized in a range of contexts. The DfES *Five Year Strategy* stated:

> As we put more emphasis on those in the system leading reform, we will increasingly need leaders (and leadership teams) with the creativity, imagination and inspiration to lead transformation. (DfES/Ofsted, 2004c, page 107)

> And all of this depends . . . in particular [on] a reshaped role for Local Government and for my Department, moving away from direction towards an enabling and empowering role. It depends on freedom for those at the front line to personalise services and to improve them. And it depends on Ministers like me holding our nerve and being able to resist the lure of the next initiative in favour of a system that drives its own improvement more and more. (DfES/Ofsted, 2004c, page 3)

Fullan (2005) reinforces this perspective:

> . . . leaders at the systems level need to engage other levels so that policies and strategies are shaped and reshaped, and the emerging bigger picture is constantly communicated and critiqued. Local leaders for their part must push outward to lead lateral capacity building and vertical exchanges with high levels of the system as a whole. (page 44)

> We need fundamental changes in the cultures of organizations and systems; the new work is harder to do, requiring much more sophistication – leaders working to change conditions, including the development of other leaders to reach a critical mass. This is the new work of leaders for sustainability . . . Enter the new leaders, starting at the school level. (page 52)

These views point to a very different model of leadership – one that is extended beyond the school, highly interactive both horizontally (with other schools and agencies) and vertically (with local authorities and national policy-makers) and engaged in the communication and critique of policies and strategies, and developing capacity across the system as a whole. Hopkins (2005) gives this approach a clear visual representation, as shown in Figure 2.1.

The crucial component of this model is the movement from dependency to interdependency as being the only way to achieve high excellence and high equity –

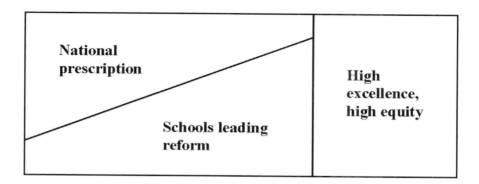

**Dependency
prescription**

National
prescription

Schools leading
reform

High
excellence,
high equity

**Interdependency
Professionalism**

Figure 2.1 From control to partnership

which in many ways is the *raison d'être* of this initiative. School leadership in the 1990s in England might be characterized as a period of high dependency; policy was largely formulated at national level and it was the responsibility of school leaders to implement it at institutional level. Obvious examples are the National Literacy and Numeracy Strategies which were formulated on the basis of perceived best practice, they were then resourced and finally disseminated. They were characterized by high degrees of specificity and virtually no local initiative or discretion. In many, though limited, respects this strategy worked; but, as has been demonstrated in Chapter 1, it is no longer doing so. The top-down approach can be seen as having created dependency in schools, i.e. a loss of confidence and lack of initiative. Education policy in England since 2004 has focused on building capacity at school level and combining central direction with local discretion, with school leaders taking on increasing responsibility for policy formulation and implementation.

The notion of 'schools leading reform' provides a significant clue as to the possible components of system leadership. It would be a naive category mistake to see system leadership as a single entity and, given the British penchant for hierarchy, a new 'level' of leadership. It needs to be seen rather as a portfolio of activities that have one thing in common – they involve leadership 'beyond the school', i.e. over and above the traditional institutionally focused roles and activities of headteachers and school leaders. The British tradition of headship can be traced back to the public schools of the nineteenth century – the tradition of Arnold and Thring – highly personalized leadership based on personal and institutional autonomy with commensurate authority. This model was adopted by the state system to the extent that headship in England is almost uniquely autonomous and accountable with an extraordinarily high degree of personal identification of the individual headteacher with the school. This has been modified in recent years by the growth of the concept of the school leadership team and moves towards shared and distributed leadership but the dominant culture is that of the headteacher responsible for the effectiveness of the individual school.

The prevailing hegemony of the past generation of educational policy-making and school leadership has been the concept of school improvement and its related model of school effectiveness. One significant outcome of this orthodoxy has been the emphasis on the integrity of the individual institution. When this is combined with an accountability model that focuses on individual school performance in a comparative setting, i.e. league tables and a 'market economy' based on parental choice, then it is hardly surprising that institutional integrity and a culture of competition should inform the nature of school leadership. This might be seen as akin to the 'territorial imperative' that informs much animal behaviour. There are also echoes of Putnam's (2000) model of bonding and bridging. He uses the concept of bonding to describe the community that is essentially introverted, self-referential and homogeneous. This is a vital characteristic of any community but it can lead to isolationism and inappropriate autonomy and exclusivity. For a community to thrive it is necessary to bond and to bridge. Bridging involves becoming inclusive, interdependent and heterogeneous. In many ways, the traditional focus of school leadership has been on bonding; system leadership requires a movement to bridging.

It would be a mistake to imagine that headteachers had no involvement outside their own schools, although it has been highly variable (and therein is the problem); headteachers have always had responsibility for, and engagement with, matters over and above the integrity of their own school. However, this was often on an 'opting-in' or representative basis. The primary focus of leadership activity, professional expectations and models of accountability saw leadership of the individual school as the key defining characteristic of headship. It would be naive to underestimate the challenge implicit in moving from an institutional focus to a systems approach; although such a movement is both inevitable and necessary.

Defining system leadership

There is no single authoritative definition of system leadership in education available and it is probably right that this is the case. Our understanding of system leadership needs to be seen as emergent and subject to a range of policies and initiatives that will see its form change over time. In its analysis of the current state of school leadership in England, PricewaterhouseCoopers (2007) argue that system leadership:

> . . . embraces all the different roles that heads can assume beyond the boundaries of their own school, i.e. those that contribute to the educational system at a local, regional or national level. It includes, for example, National Leaders of Education assuming roles that include providing advice to Government and 'virtual heads' responding to schools facing specific challenging circumstances. (page 10)

It is possible to identify a number of characteristics that allow for a cautious discussion of the present state of understanding:

> System leadership involves a shift in mindset for school leaders, emphasising what they share with others over how they differ. Where they can, system leaders eschew 'us and them' relationships – with their community, with other schools and professionals and with the DfES – and model a commitment to the learning of every child. (Innovation Unit et al., 2007, page 3)

Although it is a crude typology, it might be helpful to think of a movement in recent years from school management through school leadership to educational or system leadership:

> System leadership maximises the influence and effect of leadership across a system. It represents both a shift in the practice of leaders to ensure wider influence and in the system itself to make this possible. The result is to break down some of the false distinctions between policy and practice, creating a system better able to learn, improve and secure leverage for its outstanding leaders. (Innovation Unit, et al., 2007, page 3)

According to the paper produced by the Innovation Unit, NCSL and Demos (2007) there are three broad components to system leadership:

1 Building sustainable capacity in institutions so as to enable engagement across the system – it is clearly fundamental to any model of systems engagement that the participant's school should not be compromised

2 Developing sustainable capacity beyond the institution – developing new alliances and resources to enable systems approaches.

3 Creating a climate of professional generosity and exchange in which leaders open up professional practice to wide scrutiny and make professional learning public. (page 4)

These broad components can be developed into a model which identifies the specific functions that can be associated with system leadership. There is no statutory basis to system leadership as a generic model; it is a collective term to encompass a wide range of parallel initiatives that have the potential to transform current models of thinking about leadership in education.

Table 2.1 A typology of system leadership

8	Advising on national policies and strategies	Direct involvement with DfES through associations, think tanks, advisory bodies
7	Collaborating with other agencies	Working in the context of the Children Act
6	Working for local authorities	Advisory work, consultant leaders, school improvement partners, guidance on policy
5	Leading community initiatives	Active partnership and involvement across community initiatives
4	Leading networks, clusters and federations	Varying degrees of responsibility and authority working with other schools
3	Executive leadership	Direct involvement in the leadership of a second or third school
2	Leadership of extended services	Changing responsibility in terms of time, resources, space and activity
1	School leadership	Focus on school improvement

It is very important to reiterate that the representation of system leadership above is not intended to be hierarchical; it is rather an indication of a movement away from the traditional role, functions, behaviours and expectations of school leaders. Figure 2.1 describes what can be understood as the current taxonomy of system leadership. Equally, it is important to reinforce the point that system leadership is not a matter of career development or promotion. Every headteacher will be a system leader to some extent. For example, on current plans every school will be involved in extended services by 2010; therefore, by definition, every headteacher and many deputy and assistant heads will be involved in system leadership. Figure 2.2 is perhaps a more appropriate representation of how we might understand system leadership. The eight components can be seen as a complex interaction of a number of variables which will change according to context. A system leader will function in a number of the components of the model at the same time.

Each of these components of system leadership will be discussed in detail in the chapters that follow; at this stage it is intended only to provide brief definitions to clarify the nature of the change that is being described in our understanding of leadership in education.

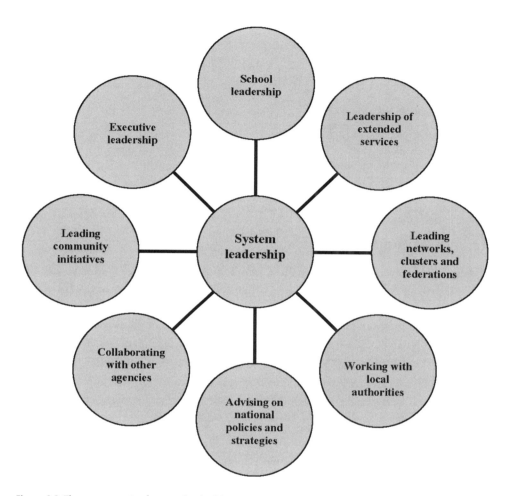

Figure 2.2 The components of system leadership

School leadership

No school leader will be unaffected by the emergence of system leadership. At the very least, all school leaders will be involved in varying degrees in the implementation and management of extended services. There is also a high probability that all school leaders will be involved in networks, clusters and federations with different levels of engagement and commitment. A related implication for every school will be the development of internal capacity through shared and distributed leadership so as to enable participation in the various aspects of system leadership.

Leadership of extended services

Current strategies require that every school will be engaged in the provision of extended services by 2010. The implications of this may be summarized as:

- Working with a range of agencies to provide additional services using the school site and resources.
- Employing additional staff to extend the school's provision beyond traditional patterns and timescales.
- Engaging with the community to identify needs and wants.
- Deploying staff to lead and manage new initiatives.

Executive leadership

This will probably involve the smallest number of school leaders. In essence, this involves the headteacher, and possibly other senior staff, from a successful school taking on direct, i.e. executive, responsibility for the day-to-day leadership and management of a school perceived to be in need of external intervention and support. This approach can cover a spectrum from critical friendship to full secondment for a specified period, with appropriate adjustments in the leadership structure of the 'donor' school.

Leading networks, clusters and federations

At this stage of the discussion, a network may be defined as an informal, voluntary association that is focused on a particular strategy or area of common interest, which has no implications in terms of internal school structures or formal accountability. A cluster is a more formal and structured relationship in which there is a clear merging and integration of a number of school roles and functions, sharing of services and staff and collaboration on innovations or policy initiatives. Hence, a group of schools might agree to develop an integrated continuing professional development (CPD) strategy by pooling budgets, developing shared provision and integrating resources. Federation is a formal change in the legal status of a number of schools so that they develop a common identity. The movement from autonomous institution through networks and clusters to federations requires a parallel shift in the scope of leadership and the perceived components of the role.

Leading community initiatives

This is probably the least defined of the elements of system leadership, simply because it represents the greatest reorientation in thinking. A useful way of understanding it would be to think of the educational leader as social entrepreneur, i.e.

seeing leadership as being actively involved in social and political action in order to change a community. This might involve local campaigns, community renewal projects and strategies to develop social capital, community coherence and redress obvious social injustices. For the Audit Commission (2006):

> This means taking positive action to counter the negative educational experiences of many parents and seeking to break the cycle of low aspiration and low attainment. (page 19)

Working with local authorities

There is a long tradition of headteachers contributing to the work of the local authority in a variety of capacities. In the past this was almost invariably with the education authority; today, with the advent of Children and Young People's Services, the role is more complex. There is a range of activities that have fallen into this category:

- secondment to the local authority (LA) to lead specific initiatives
- acting in an advisory capacity
- providing support for other headteachers as mentor/coach
- contributing to consultative panels.

Collaborating with other agencies

This is a reflection of a fundamental premise of the Children Act 2004 (Houses of Parliament, 2004) – the duty to collaborate. This is probably the least understood of the components of system leadership, as it is still emergent. Potentially it might include the following activities:

- working collaboratively on local projects related to aspects of *Every Child Matters*
- developing strategies to integrate provision
- shared developmental activities
- contributing to the leadership of integrated teams working in localities
- developing schools as local centres for Children and Young People's Services.

Advising on national policies and strategies

Headteachers have long been asked to meet the minister and have tea at 10 Downing Street. What is now emerging is a far more systematic and transparent approach to consultation. The professional associations now work in a highly sophisticated way with central government with active collaboration in the development and implementation of policy.

The implications of system leadership

The typology in Table 2.1 could be seen as a series of concentric circles or waves moving from a central point – i.e. leadership in education moving through a series of stages, each one further removed from the traditional model of headship. Another way to picture this would be as a vector with each stage representing a further step away from the school (as outlined in Figure 2.3).

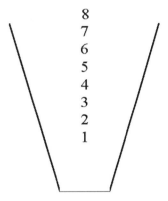

Figure 2.3 The scope of system leadership

The movement through the stages from level 1 to level 8 is characterized by a number of factors, each of which demonstrates the movement away from traditional models of headship and school leadership.

- Fewer opportunities for direct control: generally system leaders will not have the same situational authority that is associated with headship. They will not have the same leadership status and management structures to enact their decisions.
- Greater emphasis on negotiation and influence: although all effective school leaders work through negotiation and influence rather than the direct exercise of authority, they do have the potential of enforcement through contractual relationships. In many situations, system leaders will not have the same contractual status.
- Increasingly vague accountability: the accountabilities of school leaders in England are clear and explicit. Formal, contractual, professional and moral accountabilities are well understood and underpin all working relationships. Such clarity will not always be available to system leaders.

- Increasing uncertainty and ambiguity: from level 3 system leadership onwards there is a growing lack of clarity in terms of roles, relationships, structures and outcomes. The clarity and focus of school life will be increasingly replaced by more contingent situations.

- Greater potential to inform system change: as uncertainty and ambiguity increase, so does the potential to influence and inform policy at local and national level.

- Less direct involvement with school: one of the very real implications of system leadership is the loss of the sense of identity with a particular school and the professional fulfilment that most headteachers derive from their long-term commitment to the effectiveness, performance and improvement of their school.

- Working in the context of more diffuse outcomes: system leadership implies diminishing confidence about impact as the potential to exercise direct control lessens and the outcomes become more system wide and less focused on specific institutions.

These changes might be best represented by the model shown in Figure 2.4.

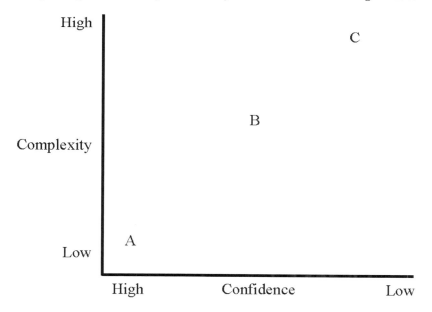

Figure 2.4 Leading beyond the school
Source: West-Burnham et al. (2007, page 126)

The traditional work of an experienced and successful headteacher might be characterized as high confidence and low complexity (point A); the components of successful school leadership are well known and understood, and there are few situations that represent a significant professional challenge. There are real opportunities to make a significant difference and personal initiatives are likely to be carried through to fruition. However, the movement to point B and beyond may well represent an increase in the complexity of the activities undertaken and a consequent reduction in confidence, unless appropriate development strategies are in place. In essence, as in all learning and development, point A is always moving and effective leaders need to be able to recognize the ever changing relationship between complexity and confidence.

It may be helpful to see this as a journey with an ever-receding horizon. The sea-trade routes of antiquity tended to follow the coastline – to aid navigation and provide shelter from storms and pirates. It was an act of considerable courage to move out of sight of land, away from the certainties of known landmarks, routines and procedures. It was also a well known fact that the horizon marked the edge of the world and sailing too close to it raised the possibility of falling off. There will be those who argue that the movement to system leadership provides a similar danger. A major issue in the implementation of system leadership will be the acceptance of a new paradigm of leadership, a different mental map of what it means to be an educational leader in addition to being a school leader.

For Hargreaves and Fink (2006):

> The hardest part of sustainable leadership is the part that provokes us to think beyond our own schools and ourselves. It is the part that calls us to serve the public good of all people's children within and beyond our community and not only the private interests of those who subscribe to our own institution. Sustainable leadership means caring for *all* the people our actions and choices affect – those whom we can't immediately see as well as those whom we can. . . . Sustainable leadership is socially just leadership, nothing simpler, nothing less. (page 158)

As with all significant changes, there will inevitably be a transitional phase in which the new and old orders overlap, and this will raise contradictions and tensions. The most obvious example of this will be the issue of accountability. The potential problem is that the old model of accountability, highly personal and focused on institutional performance, will overlap with the new model of leadership and will, potentially, compromise the integrity of the systems approach. As long as heads are accountable for their own school then, morally and professionally, that will have to take priority. At the time of going to press there is little evidence of an alternative model of accountability emerging that reflects the more diffuse and complex relationships involved in systems approaches. One of the most significant implications of the move towards system leadership is the potential tension between old and new models of leadership and their related accountability model.

This situation might be seen as two tectonic plates grinding against each other until the tension becomes so great that a rift occurs. The development of appropriate models of accountability that recognize the changing imperatives of the education system is thus an urgent priority and one that will be returned to throughout this book.

It is sometimes argued that the move from deputy to headteacher is one of the most significant changes in role – the move from headteacher to system leader may be of a greater order of magnitude given the changing scope of the work involved in this chapter in response to the issues identified in Chapter 1.

3

Every Child Matters – cooperation and collaboration

The food would be cold and would be given to her on a piece of plastic while she was tied up in the bath. She would eat it like a dog, pushing her face to the plate. Except, of course, that a dog is not usually tied up in a plastic bag full of its excrement. (Neil Garnham QC at the Victoria Climbié inquiry)

The *Laming Inquiry Report*

On 26 February 2000, England awoke to a scandal, the repercussions of which few reading the newspapers over breakfast that morning could even begin to understand. The day before, at St Mary's Hospital, Paddington, eight-year-old Victoria Climbié had died following months of unbelievable cruelty at the hands of her aunt and her partner. Victoria had been born in the Ivory Coast in November 1991. She was the fifth of seven children and apparently led a happy early childhood. After spending some time in France, she arrived in England in April 1999. Ten months later she was dead.

Lord Laming was charged with leading the inquiry into the circumstances surrounding her death. The report was published in January 2003.

The report is critical of just about every service involved and the way it was provided. It is particularly critical of the lack of cooperation and collaboration on the part of the public services involved. For anyone responsible for providing services for children and young people, the Victoria Climbié Inquiry Report was a real wake-up call. In it Lord Laming concluded:

The Report is a vivid demonstration of poor practice within and between social services, the police and the health agencies. It is also a stark reminder of the consequences of ineffective and inept management. Too often it seemed that too much time was spent deferring to the needs of Kouao and Manning, and not enough time was spent on protecting a vulnerable and defenceless child. (page 13)

Every Child Matters

The report sent shockwaves through Whitehall. The response to the inquiry from the government was rapid and the vision it contained stunning. In September 2003, the government published the Green Paper, *Every Child Matters*. The then Prime Minister, Tony Blair, stated the intention in his introduction:

> We are proposing here a range of measures to reform and improve children's care – crucially, for the first time ever requiring local authorities to bring together in one place under one person services for children, and at the same time suggesting real changes in the way those we ask to do this work carry out their tasks on our and our children's behalf . . . we want to maximise the opportunities open to them – to improve their life chances, to change the odds in their favour. So in addition, this Green Paper puts forward ideas on a number of related issues, including parenting, fostering, young people's activities and youth justice. (HM Treasury, 2003, pages 1–2)

The *Every Child Matters* (ECM) agenda sets out five outcomes for children and young people based on consultation with children and young people. These are:

- **being healthy:** enjoying good physical and mental health, and living a healthy lifestyle
- **staying safe:** being protected from harm and neglect
- **enjoying and achieving:** getting the most out of life and developing the skills for adulthood
- **making a positive contribution:** being involved with the community and society and not engaging in antisocial or offending behaviour
- **economic well-being:** not being prevented by economic disadvantage from achieving their full potential in life.

In order to support the vision, the government set about undertaking a review of public services to see what more they could do to improve parenting and family support. These included the universal services such as schools, health, social services and childcare as well as targeted and specialist support to parents of children requiring such additional support.

Underpinning this review was the concept of personalization and greater involvement by stakeholders in developing and working with the services they required.

There was a strong belief developing that services existed to meet the needs of recipients rather than designed for the benefit of the provider. In other words, the ECM agenda required a major cultural change if the vision was to be realized.

The government was able to point to progress made post 1997 and suggest that the majority of children and young people had access to better education, health and other opportunities than children and young people in previous generations. However, it remained concerned that there were still too many children and young people who were underachieving, exposed to crime, abuse and neglect, or who suffered from physical and mental health problems. The follow-up document – *Every Child Matters: Next Steps* – published in February 2004, stated categorically:

> Many children, young people and their families want and deserve a better deal. Children and young people want to feel listened to and respected. They want services that adapt to their needs, talents and circumstances. They want society to value children and the experience of childhood both in its own right, and as a preparation for adult life. Parents want more opportunities to support their children, and combine caring responsibilities with work. All of this will help families move out of poverty and prevent disadvantage being handed down from one generation to the next. (DfES, 2004a, page 26)

Since the publication of the Green Paper in 2003, there has been considerable public debate and action at both government and local level designed to realize the vision. This has been matched with considerable financial investment. Gradually, a joined-up system of health, family support, childcare and education services is developing and, at local authority level, each authority now has a director of children's services which encompasses both education and other children's and families' services such as social services and leisure. In addition, Children's Trusts are being developed in each local authority, which involves all key providers including the community and voluntary sector. The publication of *Every Child Matters: Change for Children* (DfES, 2004b) set out a range of measures for organizations providing services to children, such as schools, hospitals and the police. The idea was to enable them to work together and share information, so that all children, and especially those from vulnerable groups, have the support they need.

In order to help make the vision a reality by the time of the publication of *Every Child Matters: Change for Children* key legislation in the form of the Children Act 2004 (Houses of Parliament, 2004) had already been passed through parliament. The Act promised far reaching changes, which are dealt with in the next section.

The Children Act 2004

The Act (Houses of Parliament, 2004) is the legislative spine on which is built the reforms of children's services. It establishes for England:

- a children's commissioner, charged with championing the views and interests of children and young people
- a duty on local authorities to make arrangements to promote cooperation between agencies and other appropriate bodies (such as voluntary and community organizations) in order to improve children's well-being, and a duty on key partners to take part in the cooperation arrangements
- a duty on key agencies to safeguard and promote the welfare of children
- a duty on local authorities to set up Local Safeguarding Children Boards and on key partners to take part
- provision for databases containing basic information about children and young people, to enable better sharing of information
- a requirement for a Children and Young People's Plan to be drawn up by each local authority
- a requirement on local authorities to appoint a director of children's services and designate a lead member
- the creation of an integrated inspection framework and the conduct of joint area reviews to assess local areas' progress in improving outcomes
- provisions relating to foster care, private fostering and the education of children in care.

The 2004 Act changes the relationships between provider and recipient to an extent never existing before. The concept of personalization is now a reality and needs to be built in by the provider. It can be easily monitored – the structures are in place but the challenge remains to make these changes operational and avoid another Victoria Climbié scenario. But the agenda has gone beyond Victoria Climbié. It is no longer about avoiding another tragedy, although that, of course, is part of it; it is more about making a positive difference to the life chances of all children and young people.

Early years

A vital part of the ECM agenda begins with pregnancy. The stated intention is to create a joined-up system of health, family support, childcare and education services, so that all children get the best start possible in those important early years. By 2010, the plan is to have 3,500 children's centres established, one for each identified community in England. The ten year childcare strategy sets out four key aims (HM Treasury et al., 2004):

- **Choice and flexibility** – the aim is to ensure that all parents have a greater choice about balancing work and family life. This is about choice – not forcing parents into work who do not wish to be there. It is about providing opportunities for both parents to work or for single parents to work, secure in the knowledge that their children are safe and engaged in productive activities.

- **Availability** – for all families with children aged up to 14 who need it, an affordable, flexible, high-quality childcare place that meets their circumstances. For 11 to 14 year olds, more parents are likely to depend on a varied menu of activities in a safe place to be provided through extended services in schools. This is planned to operate on an all year around basis. It is likely that many primary schools will provide a similar offer for children from eight years of age. Arrangements for children eight years of age and under will need to be more formal.

- **Quality** – high-quality provision with a highly skilled childcare and Early Years workforce. The strategy sets out to ensure that such provision will be among the best in the world.

- **Affordability** – families to be able to afford flexible, high-quality childcare that is appropriate for their needs. It is already possible for couples or single parents to claim this benefit as long as they meet certain criteria. This tax credit, which is aimed at childcare, is not just for low income families or single parents, but covers, at least to some extent, most of the working population. It is weighted, however, towards the lower income brackets.

Currently all children between the ages of three and five years are entitled to 12.5 hours a week for 38 weeks of the year of free education. This education is based on the Foundation Stage curriculum, which since 2002 has been part of the National Curriculum. From September 2010 the entitlement will increase to 15 hours a week over the 38 weeks of the normal school year. The Foundation Stage curriculum is different than that used for children and young people in statutory education in that it focuses on six areas of development rather than a subject focus. The six areas of development are:

1 personal, social and emotional development

2 communication, language and literacy

3 mathematical development

4 knowledge and understanding of the world

5 physical development

6 creative development.

However, this is not viewed as the total answer for Early Years and, in 2007, a new framework was published that sets out not only the statutory framework for both education and care for children affected but also the requirements on providers both in the public and private sectors. This framework can be found online at www.standards.dfes.gov.uk/primary/publications/foundation_stage/eyfs/

This statutory framework is explained in the following way:

> The Early Years Foundation Stage (EYFS) is a comprehensive framework which sets the standards for learning, development and care of children from birth to 5. It builds on and will replace the existing statutory Curriculum Guidance for the Foundation Stage, the non-statutory Birth to Three Matters framework, and the regulatory frameworks in the National Standards for Under 8s Day Care and Childminding. All registered early years providers and schools will be required to use the EYFS from September 2008. (DCSF, 2007a)

Matters have come a long way since the Sure Start programme, with the aim 'to deliver the best start in life for every child', launched in 1999. As of September 2007, there are almost 1,600 children's centres throughout England with at least one in every authority except Rutland and the Isles of Scilly.

Children's centres are an important concept because they offer a wide range of multi-agency services for children and their families. These centres are key to the strategy to deliver better outcomes for children and families. They are also a vital part of the childcare strategy.

Youth matters

In July 2005, the government published the *Youth Matters* Green Paper (DfES, 2005a), which set out a new deal for young people. The aims underpinning the Green Paper are to provide all young people with:

- More things to do and places to go in their local area, including greater choice and more say over what services are available.
- Increased opportunities to partake in voluntary services, as well as other ways to make a meaningful contribution to their local community.
- Better information, advice and guidance about issues that matter to them, in a more accessible way and in such a way that is of interest to their age group.
- Better support when they need extra assistance to deal with the issues and crises they might face. The best known example is targeted youth support, which is designed to detect problems early and provide the necessary interventions.

Targeted youth support it designed to support young people who are likely to need support and access to a range of opportunities from the plethora of agencies, public, private or voluntary, which exist to support them. Only in this way is it felt that the necessary help and guidance can be provided in a timely, coordinated and effective way. Ultimately it is intended that more young people, particularly the most vulnerable, should have a better chance to enjoy their lives, build a more positive future for themselves and avoid serious problems later in their lives. Services involved include, but are not restricted to, behaviour support, child and adolescent mental health services (CAMHS), connections, counselling services, drugs and alcohol services, education welfare, health services, housing and housing support, information advice and guidance providers, the police, schools, social services, sexual health services, teenage parent support workers, voluntary and community sector agencies, youth offending services and youth services. In order to support this programme new systems are being put in place, including the Common Assessment Framework (CAF) and ContactPoint (an information sharing index). These systems are designed to promote more effective, earlier identification of additional needs and to speed up the process for intervention from targeted services.

The *Youth Matters* agenda is not limited to young people who may need additional support. There is a growing market for positive activities for young people (PAYP). These tend to be classified as either structured or unstructured activities. Structured activities tend to cover those activities that are formally organized and might include sports activities, clubs and voluntary activities. Such activities are designed to have clear health, learning or social and personal development aims. They may be offered through extended services in schools or through organizations away from the school site. They enable young people to participate in, or initiate, planned and purposeful activity voluntarily. Unstructured activities are those activities that young people choose to engage in during their leisure time, for example music events, cinema or more active pursuits.

The aim of providing more positive activities for young people is to ensure that they have something productive available that they enjoy doing, rather than becoming bored and possibly drifting into crime as a result. There is a belief that the availability of constructive things to do will develop young people as good citizens and will develop their aspirations, confidence and leadership skills for later in life.

According to the consultation following *Youth Matters*:

- 68 per cent of young people would like to help decide how local councils spend money on providing activities for young people
- 71 per cent of young people said they would do up to four hours of activities in their spare time if they had the opportunity

- 73 per cent of young people thought that having more places for young people to go would stop some teenagers getting into trouble

- 83 per cent of adults/organizations and 85 per cent of young people supported proposals for empowering young people to shape local services

- 83 per cent of young people thought that a card that gave discounts and money to spend on activities would encourage them to do more in their spare time. However, while 33 per cent of adults/organizations agreed with the proposal to introduce an opportunity card, 46 per cent were unconvinced. (DfES, 2006, page 9)

For the *Youth Matters* agenda to work, not only are the cooperation and participation of young people required but it is also heavily dependent on young people having both the voice to say what they want and the leadership skills to make things happen. This requires the willingness of adults to listen and also the willingness of adults to facilitate this happening, particularly in schools. While the pupil voice is not a new idea, the empowerment of young people has grown exponentially over the past ten years. One example is the Young People's Parliament which came into existence in 1997 but more accessible to most children and young people are pupil councils in schools. The National College for School Leadership (NCSL) has developed a student leadership programme as part of the London Challenge, in the belief that the greater engagement of young people in the process is central to the ECM agenda and the raising of achievement. The programme is designed to provide the skills, confidence and motivation for young people to engage directly in improving their school.

Children in care

There are many groups of children and young people in our society who have the potential to be more vulnerable than their peers. These include children and young people who have a disability, whose first language is not English, who have special educational needs, or who come from economically deprived or dysfunctional family structures, to name some. One of the most vulnerable groups is that of children whose corporate parents are local authorities, that is, children in care (or looked after children).

The White Paper *Care Matters: Time for Change* (DfES, 2007) points out that:

- In 2006, only 12 per cent of children in care achieved 5 A*-C grades at GCSE (or equivalent) compared to 59 per cent of all children.

- Their health is poorer than that of other children. Forty-five per cent of children in care are assessed as having a mental health disorder compared with around 10 per cent of the general population.

- Over 50 per cent of children in care responding to *Care Matters* said that they had difficulties accessing positive activities.
- Of children in care aged 10 or over, 9.6 per cent were cautioned or convicted for an offence during the year – almost three times the rate for all children of this age.
- Thirty per cent of care leavers aged 19 were not in education, employment or training (NEET).

At any one stage there are around 60,000 children in care, either with foster parents or in residential homes. Many face disruption to their schooling as they are moved from one care arrangement to another. They do not necessarily have access to the best schools in an area since they can often move mid-year. Friendships can be difficult to develop, mitigating against their social and emotional development. And they can often feel that they are not wanted or do not belong.

The intention of the White Paper is to bring about a change in the way children and young people in care are treated, using a range of measures. These include ensuring that, as they are likely to be taken into care, they have more support and that there is more effective support for all aspects of children in care's lives outside school. There are to be increased responsibilities for corporate parents and increased powers. Corporate parents will have the right to a place in the most suitable school for that child, whether or not that school is already full. There will be more support for children in care, covering the transition period into adulthood. And accountability systems will be strengthened including Ofsted being given greater powers to monitor what is actually happening on the ground. Each child in care will have a 'virtual headteacher', championing his or her cause in school – another form of system leadership.

As one child in care has suggested:

> I would like equality to happen throughout, whether it be to fostered children or to all children in general. But special circumstances must be made for children that are in care or fostered so that the gap does not widen. (Collarbone, 2007, page 6)

Leadership in an ECM context

The final section of this chapter focuses on leadership in an ECM context. To date, this chapter has focused briefly on the what and why behind this agenda, including consideration of three key areas: Early Years, targeted youth support and children in care. The authors have deliberately avoided too much reference to extended services in schools because this is dealt with in Chapter 4. For more detail on the ECM agenda it is worth visiting the website at www.everychildmatters.gov.uk/

The ECM agenda is more dependent on multi-agency working than perhaps any other agenda operating currently in England. This is against a background of not only the changing nature of the society within which we live, but also a changing social structure that means there are more disparate family units, greater complexity across the whole of our social structure and more pressure on children's centres and schools to equip children and young people for the twenty-first century.

This book is targeted, although not exclusively, at school leaders, so this section focuses on the impact this may have for leadership in schools. As explained earlier and in more detail later, how we use our schools and the resources, including the human resources within them, form the key lever for shifting the opportunities and challenges for children and young people. In order to drive forward the ECM agenda there needs to be a refocus on the requirements for those seen as leaders in the system – particularly those in school leadership contexts. The notion, for example, that multi-agency working works because many people think that it is a good idea and their hearts are in the right place is simply nonsensical. Agencies, including schools, have their own cultures, agendas, language and aims, each of which will be very different despite the commitment of the people involved in trying to make the agenda work. The leadership required in this scenario is very different than the leadership required in a single organizational structure. In other words, we are again moving into a system leadership model.

However, there are challenges that need to be addressed in order to make both the new realities and the leadership requirements a reality. Recently the Training and Development Agency for Schools (TDA) and NCSL began to work together to address the question why existing school leaders buy into (or do not buy into) the ECM/extended schools (ES) agenda. As part of the development of the programme, the researchers from the University of Warwick involved noted that leaders of extended schools required the following skills (Harris et al., 2007):

- negotiation
- change management
- brokerage ability
- interpersonal skills
- team building capability
- ability to manage risk
- financial acumen
- contextual literacy.

For most of the roles (as we suggested in Chapter 2) that system leaders might undertake, this set of skills presents a useful starting point. System leaders are required in order to bring about system change. System change depends on people. Therefore it is not surprising that effective system leaders are able to lead and manage change but, perhaps more importantly, are very skilful when dealing with people and are also able to develop useful networks. They are very emotionally intelligent.

Daniel Goleman et al. (2002) explained this succinctly, so perhaps we should leave the final word in this chapter to him and his colleagues.

> No matter what leaders set out to do – whether it's creating strategy or mobilizing teams to action – their success depends on *how* they do it. Even if they get everything else just right, if leaders fail in this primal task of driving emotions in the right direction, nothing they do will work as well as it could or should. (page 3)

4 Leading extended services in an educational setting

This is a demanding, but exciting vision. It is a vision which fits with what parents want for their children, with the direction that schools are already moving in and with the Government's wider Every Child Matters objectives of ensuring that children stay safe, are healthy, enjoy and achieve, make a positive contribution and achieve economic wellbeing. Schools, located as they are right at the heart of the community, are ideally placed to take up this challenge. (DfES, 2005c, page 4)

What is an extended school?

The development of extended schools is a key part of the DCSF vision to meet the requirement of the government's *Every Child Matters: Change for Children* (DfES, 2004b) agenda. It is an essential driver of a wider transformation of the way that children's services can work together. It is a recognition that schools are often at the heart of children and young people's lives and equally likely to be at the heart of the community they live in. Traditionally they have also been, in many cases, an expensive, underused community resource. The extended schools agenda builds on the idea that schools are ideally placed to offer access to a range of extended services that can have a positive impact on standards and the life chances of children, young people, their families and the communities in which they live.

Effective extended services can help children overcome barriers to learning and enrich the curriculum. These same services can improve access to public services vital to the well-being of the child. They can provide safe and productive childcare so that parents have more flexibility in their working lives. They can provide opportunities for parents to help them understand better the learning needs of their children and help the parents with their own learning. They can help communities gain greater access to the resources that the school has at its disposal.

The current agenda sets out an entitlement for all children and young people to be in place by 2010. This proposes that schools should be providing access to the following services by then:

- **Primary schools provide access to high-quality childcare** combined with a varied menu of activities (study support) to enhance achievement and broaden interests, 8.00am–6.00pm, five days a week, 48 weeks a year, in accordance with their communities' needs.

- **Secondary schools provide access to a varied menu of study support and enrichment activities**, which provide fun and stimulating activities for young people, as well as a safe place to be.

- **Schools provide access to parenting support**, including information sessions for parents of pupils joining Reception and on transfer to secondary school; signposting to national and local sources of information, advice and support; access to parenting groups using structured, evidence-based parenting programmes; and family learning sessions to allow children to learn with their parents, where consultation has shown there is a demand.

- **Swift and easy access**: working closely with other statutory services and the voluntary and community sectors, schools ensure that children with additional needs are identified as early as possible, and are well supported through integrated working with other services.

- **Schools ensure they provide community access** to appropriate facilities, such as ICT suites, sports and arts facilities, and also provide access to adult learning.

Many schools may choose to develop an even richer mix of services and activities. These are already found in full service extended schools (FSES) which have existed since 2003 and were pathfinders for extended schools. At least one FSES exists in each authority and these schools received additional funding in order to set up comprehensive multi-agency provision and services. Although there is not inconsiderable funding available to set-up and sustain extended schools, the key to future development depends on: a) a school's and LA's commitment to the agenda; and b) the willingness of governing bodies to use the new powers they have as a result of the Education Act 2002 in order to ensure future sustainability.

The concept of extending the school day is not a new issue for a large number of schools in England. The vast majority of schools are used to providing additional opportunities for their pupils which include breakfast clubs, lunchtime activities and after-school activities, including sport, ICT and 'catch-up' classes. School productions and other artistic activities would not be possible without a clear commitment on the part of both adults and children (and young people) to after-school and even Saturday activity. Many teachers have always been willing to provide some form of additional activity, usually related to their subject or a particular interest they have, through the use of after-school clubs. In addition, schools with the necessary resources have been used by both the further education (FE) and youth service sectors in order to provide the necessary accommodation and resources at a cost effective rate. This is acknowledged within the extended schools agenda and it is this history which is providing the scaffolding on which extended schools are being built.

The Education Act 2002

The Education Act 2002 provided a new legal framework which allowed schools to take on new responsibilities with regard to extended provision. It enabled governing bodies to:

- directly provide facilities and services that benefit pupils, families and the local community
- enter into agreements with other partners to provide services on school premises
- set out minimal safeguards, for example to consult stakeholders and partners before developing services.

While the Education Act 2002 provides governing bodies with new opportunities to exploit the available resources within their schools for the benefit of the pupils, it also requires new responsibilities with regard to consultation. In other words, the extended schools agenda does not set itself up to promote competition with other schools or other providers, nor does it assume schools will be in a position to deliver the programme without partnership working with other schools and other providers, including both the public and private sector.

Throughout the country, schools are now working in close collaboration with the local primary care trust (PCT), the police, youth organizations, social services, youth offending teams and private providers in order to deliver appropriate services for their local communities on a year round basis. Local authorities are working with schools to form school clusters, so that no one school is expected to necessarily deliver all of the services itself.

Case study

Eleven Surrey schools formed the Horley Learning Partnership (HLP, 2007) in 2003, jointly appointing a part-time coordinator to help the schools work together and improve learning. The HLP's role expanded when the group of schools became Surrey's first extended schools confederation in 2005, under the initiative 'Organizing for Success – School Focused Community Planning'. Targeted holiday activities and clubs are one aspect of the HLP's work. The Partnership aims to enhance the education of all pupils and their families through collective expertise, improved coordination of professional services and the creation of an effective network, maximizing the educational opportunities for the community.

Governance of extended schools

The role of the governing body has changed dramatically since 1986 and continues to change. The concept of an extended school has brought with it new implications for the strategic leadership of schools, whether the governing body decides to run the extended school itself or whether it employs alternative governance arrangements. The governing body has the ultimate responsibility for deciding whether or not the school should be offering extended services and how it might do this. It has the power to provide, or enter into a contract or other arrangements to provide, facilities and services that 'further any charitable purpose for the benefit of pupils at the school or their families, or people who live or work in the locality in which the school is situated'.

The governing body is required to think strategically about the need for ensuring that there is coherence between the extended schools and standards agendas in terms of the school development strategy, taking account of the local Children and Young People's Plan. This means that the governing body needs a clear strategic overview of the school's extended services offer and how it relates to the core function of the school. This needs to be reflected in both the school's improvement planning and in its process of self-evaluation. This should further be reflected in the ongoing completion of the self-evaluation form (SEF).

A key to how the school operates and what it stands for is encapsulated in its vision, so it is important that the school's extended services provision is in alignment with that vision in order to promote the intended outcomes and advantages to others.

In planning and promoting extended services, the governing body will need to consider how these services will operate. In many cases these will operate through the use of different arrangements taking account of what is already available in the locality, what the school is able to provide itself and what can be achieved through working in partnership with other schools and agencies. The governing body is also responsible for ensuring that the school continues to comply with *Raising Standards and Tackling Workload: A National Agreement* (Social Partnership, 2003) and that it does not undermine efforts to improve the work–life balance of the staff in the school, particularly the gains made on behalf of the teaching staff. The governing body has a particular responsibility to ensure that the headteacher does not become overburdened.

In recent years, a number of schools have begun to employ extended schools coordinators (ESCOs) and, where schools are operating in clusters for the provision of extended services, a cluster manager. In some LAs the cluster manager is employed by the LA. The extended schools aspect of the Standards Fund for 2008 to 2011 will provide funding to help promote the growth of this role.

Another consideration for the governing body is the governance arrangements it wishes to adopt in order to deliver the services. There is likely to be a combined method of governance, depending on the services on offer, but there are four basic options available for consideration.

1 Direct management by the governing body

In this situation, extended services are provided, managed and even delivered by the school, although it may well include external providers. The governing body decides which services and facilities to provide, having consulted the LA, staff, parents, pupils and members of the community it serves. The governing body is directly accountable for the services and facilities provided. This form of governance makes it easier for the governing body to ensure that the services are run within the cultural ethos of the school and it allows the governing body to set and maintain the standards of service required. This does not mean that the governing body is directly involved in the day-to-day management and delivery of the services and this task is likely to be delegated to an ESCO employed by the school. In many cases, the staff delivering the services would be employed by the governing body or LA in the case of community and voluntary controlled schools.

Case study

In keeping with the integrated nature of the 'learning campus', Goddard Park community primary, in Swindon, has a single governing body covering both the school and children's centre, and all the extended services that are offered through them. An extended services governors' committee has been created to monitor this work, and this sits in the regular governing body structure. Representatives of two other schools in the local area have been invited to join this committee.

2 The governing body sets up a limited company

In this case, the governing body establishes a limited company and/or a charity to provide and manage the services. In these circumstances the company is the accountable body and is likely to employ many of the staff. This arrangement may well be attractive in the case of a cluster or federation of schools, or where the school sees opportunities for generating income which can then be used to support those services that do not attract a sustainable level of income but are nevertheless considered important by the school. Governors and staff at the school may well become directors of the company/charity and, in the case of a cluster, will be drawn from across the schools. The level of involvement by governors will depend on the level of control the governors wish to retain. As with the previous arrangement, this arrangement does help ensure that the services are run within the cultural ethos of the school, and the governing body is able to set and maintain the standards of service. While the directors of the company would appoint someone to manage the services, for workload reasons, this should not be the headteacher. The headteacher would need to decide whether he or she wished to be a director or to leave this role to others.

Case study

North Prospect Community School, in Plymouth, has a long tradition of partnership working with the local community, and extended services are provided through two specially created companies, both of which are majority controlled by local residents. The school has also initiated a number of health projects that led to the school getting Sure Start funding, the building of a children's centre and, most recently, the opening of a doctor's surgery on the school site. The challenge is to integrate these services within the school and out into the community.

3 The governing body works in partnership with a third-party provider

In this case, some or all of the extended services are provided and managed by another organization through a contract or agreement with the governing body. The provider could be from the private or public sector and may even be an LA provider. It is likely, for example, that childcare provision will be the responsibility of an external provider and may not necessarily be provided on the school site, although this may well be an attractive option. In this situation, the external provider is the accountable body and is responsible for ensuring that the business is viable. The advantage is that there is little additional burden placed on either the governing body or the headteacher. However, the governing body would still need to ensure that such services were of an acceptable quality and met the expectations of stakeholders and the users of the service. The LA is likely to be able to provide guidance on local providers, or the school may already have services in existence provided by third-party organizations or individuals.

> **Case study**
>
> Community and learning partnerships (CLPs) are the local delivery vehicle for delivering integrated children's services in Staffordshire. An ambitious plan that is intended to transform children's services in the county, the creation of 50 local partnerships, aims to bring together multi-agency teams to work with schools and children's centres to deliver a core offer that reflects the needs of each community.

4 A voluntary committee

In this final example, extended services are provided and managed by a voluntary committee. In this way there can be greater community involvement. The level of commitment of the governing body is a matter for it to decide. There is likely to be some participation from the school but this may be limited to ensure it is a community run project rather than dominated by the school. Such a model may be particularly attractive to a cluster of schools. In some cases, such committees have significant delegated powers, which enable them to provide an effective and efficient leadership role with regard to what services are provided and how they are delivered. Members of the committee may be appointed as associate governors, allowing final accountability to rest with the governing body while ensuring greater involvement of and ownership by the community. Such a model is likely to still involve a member of the staff of the school with responsibility for day-to-day management. However, it is likely that the governing body would still be responsible for the appointment of such a person, and this would include representatives from the voluntary committee on the appointment panel. One attraction of this model could be that the governing body does not have the same control as in models 1 and 2 and that a voluntary committee does not have the same legal obligations, or powers or levels of accountability that exist with the other models.

> **Case study**
>
> Wigan Council's strategy for extended school provision envisages clusters of schools coordinating service provision for different areas of the city. A core cluster of six schools – governed by a joint management committee – has been set up to pilot this approach.

Case study

Managing the provision of extended schools in a cluster such as Moorlands, in Staffordshire, is not simple. It requires extensive coordination between schools, service providers and others in order to work effectively. To start with, a steering group was set up with representatives from all participating schools. The group worked with other community partners and service providers to arrange basic service delivery. From this, a management advisory group was set up, which includes the steering group and other partners and agencies.

Leadership in an extended schools context

The extended schools agenda provides a new opportunity for system leadership at school level. This will not be limited to the headteacher or members of the senior leadership team but, in many cases, will include members of the governing body. It could also include, as the role develops, cluster managers whether employed by the school or the local authority. In a literature review, conducted on behalf of the NCSL, the authors identified the following aspects of extended schools in a system leadership scenario:

> Whilst ECM reforms represent the culmination of efforts to achieve more joined-up services for children, it was preceded by other policies with the same goal. **Extended schools** are one example of this, which is envisaged as using institutional bases for the delivery of a wide range of services to young people. These might include co-location on school grounds of social workers, special needs staff, youth workers and police. (O'Leary and Craig, 2007, page 10)

> **Leaders of extended schools** have begun to learn the discipline of building holistic packages of services around the needs of individuals, families and communities. Often this involves co-ordinating the offer made by one school with the activities of other schools in the area, as well as multi-agency services run by the local authority. (O'Leary and Craig, 2007, page 12)

Chapter 2 includes reference to leadership of extended schools as one scenario for a system leadership role.

Of course, the extended schools agenda does place additional pressures on many headteachers who apparently decide this is simply an additional responsibility placed on their shoulders. In other cases this is viewed in a more positive light, as a method of making a difference to the pupils served by the school. This can be equally dangerous if the headteacher involved is more focused on extended services than on the core purpose of the school. It is not such a problem if the same headteacher is able to delegate responsibilities for core purpose delivery to members of the senior leadership team while focusing on a wider stakeholder involvement.

Recent research conducted by the University of Warwick for NCSL and the TDA concluded that leadership is the key driver for change and the successful implementation of ECM and extended schools (Harris et al., 2007). The skills and abilities required by those leading the necessary change agenda have been listed in Chapter 3.

These same skills and abilities are the key skills required for a system leader but they are not necessarily the skills a governing body might focus on in appointing a member of the leadership team or, more significantly, the headteacher. In fact, Chapter 2 suggests that there is a need to include a seventh strand in the National Standards for headteachers, related to leadership of extended schools. This involves more than the requirements contained in Strand 6 – Strengthening community.

As the extended schools agenda develops over the next five years – not only to meet the needs of the communities they serve but also become financially sustainable – the role of the headteacher will change dramatically. Schools will no longer be working in isolation, as clusters, partnerships and federations develop. There is already evidence that schools working together and with their LAs and other organizations and agencies are producing the most consistently effective and sustainable extended schools. John West-Burnham has previously argued that leading extended services is a form of system leadership and, as he argued at NCSL's Leadership Network conference in 2006:

> The notion that a school can achieve all five of the ECM outcomes by itself is nonsense. It could even be argued that system leadership needs to be rooted in Every Child Matters because system leadership is not just about running more and more good schools. (quoted in Bond et al., 2006, page 3)

Case studies on the TDA extended schools website consistently point to the importance of schools working in partnership with other schools and agencies in order to achieve the outcomes that form the basis of the *Every Child Matters* agenda and, in particular, the role set out for schools through extended services (TDA, 2007).

Ofsted (2006), in its report into extended schools and children's centres, noted the importance of close cooperation between agencies and schools in the context of extended services:

> Cross-sector working was most successful when those responsible for managing and developing extended services were well informed of the remit of different agencies and how the impact of their joint working might be judged. In contrast,

weak understanding and a lack of such appreciation had a profound effect on the level of commitment and the rate of progress in developing coordinated services. (page 18)

The report went on to add:

The most effective settings required agencies to liaise and collaborate in setting up courses, advertising and staffing them. This often produced greater cost effectiveness. This was especially relevant given the short-term nature of some grants and the tapering of longer-term funding. Facilities were often provided free of charge. Shared offices for service providers at the setting also reduced costs. To improve efficiency further, agencies evaluated outcomes systematically. (page 19)

It can be seen, from what limited evidence is currently available, that the type of leadership necessary to lead extended services is different than that traditionally expected from a headteacher, where the focus is more on teaching, learning and the raising of educational achievement rather than the more holistic view of outcomes for children and young people as envisioned through the *Every Child Matters* agenda. This is a key premise outlined in both Chapters 2 and 3 of this book.

Another equally important consideration, within the context of leading extended schools, is the willingness or ability of the leaders to lead and manage change, rather than simply cope with it or hope it will go away. As argued in an earlier chapter, this stance is not a particularly effective course of action in today's educational climate. The reality is that it is no longer an option to argue that schools should just focus on teaching and learning or that they need concern themselves with only between 15 per cent and 18 per cent of a child's life. The personalization agenda and the very survival of the concept of schools as appropriate organizations for the development of the minds and well-being of children and young people as leaders and citizens for the twenty-first century require the ability of school leaders to change and adapt to a new climate of extended services and political and stakeholder expectations that goes well beyond the traditional concept of the school as recipient.

The University of Warwick's research, referred to earlier, found that there is a consistent and powerful interrelationship between workforce reform and effective ECM/ES implementation. However, the report, in one of its key findings, suggests:

Many schools find the challenges of ECM/ES overwhelming and this is the main reason for their resistance. It is clear that many of the low implementation schools do not know how to manage the change process required for the implementation of ECM/ES. They are not unwilling to implement ECM/ES but lack the vision, support, guidance and direction to make this happen.

A later chapter in this book will discuss change and workforce reform in more detail but this finding produces further evidence that, without strong and committed system leadership and schools working in collaboration, there is little chance of the vision contained within the extended schools prospectus being achieved across the system. This is despite the fact that, as of the beginning of October 2007, over 8,000 (or 37 per cent) maintained schools in England are delivering the full core offer, and this is well ahead of target. In the context of extended schools, system leadership offers a more strategic approach to improving the overall performance of the education system over time.

5 Leadership beyond the school

This chapter examines the component of system leadership that might be characterized as 'extended headship'. This phrase describes the work of headteachers, in particular, who accept responsibility, in varying degrees, for the leadership of another school or support existing leaders. As with all aspects of system leadership there is a broad continuum of involvement, with varying degrees of formal responsibility and accountability. In all cases, however, the relationship can be classified as expression of models of consultancy, mentoring and coaching, and facilitation. In essence these are various manifestations of a helping relationship, the idea that an individual with particular skills and qualities works with another to enhance their effectiveness.

This type of relationship in education might be classified in the following way:

- friends and neighbours
- mentoring schemes
- consultant leaders
- school improvement partners
- executive heads
- national leaders of education.

Friends and neighbours

This title is not intended to trivialize or diminish the importance of this relationship. It is, in fact, one of the most significant resources available to newly appointed heads and those new to a LA, and faced with new issues and challenges. Anyone who has provided inputs at headteacher conferences will acknowledge that their primary role is to fill the gaps between coffee and lunch which is where the real support and development takes place.

This aspect of support for headteachers might be best characterized as 'professional generosity'. It is the sharing of advice, expertise, experience and knowledge and works through informal networks, phone calls and meals. Its strength lies in its informal and personal nature and it would be compromised if it was formalized or structured. Local authority advisory staff will often fill a similar role (although this might be compromised by its role as School Improvement Partners – see below) or facilitate networking.

It would be a mistake to underestimate the importance of friendship in professional support. By its very nature, it implies trust, openness and confidentiality, and undoubtedly plays a significant role in enhancing the effectiveness and sustainability of school leaders.

Mentoring schemes

Notwithstanding the points made above about the importance of informal relationships, there is also a case for formal procedures to secure entitlement. Many LAs' and school leaders' professional associations provide formal and structured support, notably for new heads. Mentoring for new heads is widely recognized as one of the most powerful and high-impact strategies to provide support and maximize their effectiveness. Hobson (2003) identifies the following roles adopted by mentors of new heads:

- assisting new headteachers to solve their own problems
- acting as a catalyst or sounding board
- providing linkage to people or resources
- discussing various topics relating to school management
- offering solutions to the new headteachers' problems. (pages 1–2)

He goes on to identify the perceived advantages for new headteachers:

- benefits to their own professional development
- improved performance/problem analysis
- insights into current practice
- awareness of different approaches to headship
- increased reflectiveness
- improved self-esteem. (page 2)

There may be situations where mentoring as a generic, supportive strategy moves into coaching, where the focus is much more on specific aspects of performance and is more explicitly related to confidence and capability in specifics of the job.

Consultant leaders

This is a concept developed by the NCSL as a means of identifying headteachers and other school leaders who can contribute to the learning and development of other school leaders through a range of NCSL programmes.

The consultant leader programme works on a model of client-centred consultancy and focuses on a range of competencies and skills:

- accurate self-assessment
- self-confidence
- self-management
- empathy
- partnering
- pattern recognition
- developing others
- non-possessive warmth
- group management
- enquiry strategies
- programme design.

Consultant leaders are thus highly skilled in the development of others but are also developed themselves and thus potentially more effective in their own role and very well placed to extend their work in the broader field of system leadership.

School improvement partners (SIPs)

This role was introduced in 2004, and is pivotal to the school improvement and standards agenda. The SIP acts for the LA and is the main link with local and national strategies working to the following principles:

- **focus on pupil progress and attainment across the ability range**, and the many factors which influence it, including pupil well-being, extended services and parental involvement;
- **respect for the school's autonomy** to plan its development, starting from the school's self-evaluation and the needs of the pupils and of other members of the school community;
- **professional challenge and support**, so that the school's practice and performance are improved; and

- **evidence-based assessment** of the school's performance and its strategies for improving teaching and learning. (DCSF, 2007b, page 3)

The focus of the work as a SIP is in response to the following questions:

- How well is the school performing?
- What are the key factors?
- What are the key priorities and targets for improvement?
- How will the school achieve them? (DCSF, 2007b, page 4)

School improvement partners are, thus, for those who are headteachers – a key example of the movement from school to system leadership. In their role of providing 'professional challenge', acting as 'critical professional friend' and 'contributing to whole-school improvement' (DCSF, 2007b, page 19) they are combining professional and personal credibility with systems wide responsibility. Berry (2007) provides important insights into the role of the SIP and the headteacher working as a SIP:

> The credibility that a practising head in a school in challenging circumstances brings to the role of SIP is crucially important. . . . The impact that this can have on the education system generally could be considerable. (page 4)

> The SIP role needs to be clearly understood by all parties concerned. Professionalism and transparency are the qualities most important in this relationship. (page 4)

> For a SIP to be as effective as they could be – and for the headteacher and the school to derive maximum benefit from the new relationship – the interpersonal skills are paramount. . . . My view is that, although data is of course important, it is empowering schools to utilise the data to inform practice that is the key and this will not be done if there is distrust and a lack of transparency. (page 5)

> Above all, what I have enjoyed about my roles is that as a SIP I have been told by the headteachers that I have worked with that they have valued my contribution to their schools. This has made me feel that I was contributing to education beyond my school. (page 5)

It is this last point that confirms the potential of system leadership – contributing towards improving the whole system on the basis of professional expertise, which also benefits the individual and his or her own school.

Executive heads

This category describes the situation where a headteacher takes on direct (executive) responsibility for the leadership of another school while retaining overall responsibility for his or her own school. (The term is also used to describe the lead headteacher in a federation – this is discussed in Chapter 6.)

Executive headship usually comes about because a school finds itself in a situation where it is unable to make progress and lacks the internal capacity to put in place the appropriate strategies. Executive heads are usually approached by the local authority and the precise terms of the executive headship are negotiated according to the context and need. The remit is essentially the same in all cases: to address immediate issues, to secure rapid improvement and then to build capacity and sustainability and avoid creating a dependency culture (although there are examples of this relationship being extended into a federation or academy).

NCSL (2005a) is quite clear about the impact of executive headship on the partner school:

- speed of transformation
- transference of effective school systems from the lead school
- opportunity to be coached by high-calibre staff
- improved distributed leadership
- improved management structures
- improved behaviour and attendance
- a rigorous focus on learning and achievement:
  - high expectations
  - curriculum focus
  - professional development
- improved clarity of focus for all staff and mechanisms to support this
- a no-compromise approach to staff capability proceedings as a move towards high-quality teaching and learning provision
- the development of a 'can do' culture
- enhanced school community confidence in the potential for the school to secure improvement. (page 27)

There were also significant and tangible benefits for the lead school:

- opportunities for professional development and career development at a range of levels; heightened lead school capacity
- extended reputation of the school

- opportunities to learn from the partner school experience and reflect on implications for own school. (page 28)

There is a number of significant implications for our understanding of system leadership from the NCSL study:

- The need for whole-school leadership to be widely distributed in the lead school.
- The fact that executive headship is almost invariably executive school leadership – headteachers almost always involve senior staff in the partner school.
- The opportunity for the lead school to consolidate and extend its own successes and strengths.
- The importance of open and collaborative relationships and the centrality of trust.

What was also clear was the need for a systems perspective that transcends individual school issues, in the words of headteachers in the NCSL study:

> I still think the executive head role is helping both schools thinking strategically, not just individually but with a collaborative view. While we've got the school-to-school partnership we need to be thinking how we can both gain from that. What do they think they can get from me ... and that's also me using my networks and connections.

> As an executive head, what I can do is look strategically across both schools and look at their needs and look at what the area needs and how we can use the resources of both schools to benefit the wider community, and to not worry about who's where in the league tables and admissions, because what I realised is both schools can survive. (NCSL, 2005a, page 18)

National leaders of education (NLE)

In many ways NLEs embody much of what has already been described in Chapter 2 as the characteristics of system leaders. Their role is to:

- provide additional leadership to schools in challenging circumstances
- advise ministers and other key stakeholders on education policy
- advise NCSL on the development of potential/aspirant NLEs. (NCSL, 2007, page 4)

The specific functions of an NLE might include (for example):

- to coordinate and direct the work of the interim/acting headteacher
- to enable students to achieve outstanding results at all levels
- to develop the client school as a high 'value-added' school

- to recruit, retain and develop the best teachers, classroom assistants and education support staff
- to increase the number of applications for student places
- to raise the status of the client school in the eyes of the community
- to provide quality facilities and resources that will be used by the whole community
- to implement a training and development programme for all senior and middle leaders. (NCSL, 2007, page 24)

This is a challenging, even intimidating, list but it is an accurate reflection of what the NLEs have achieved in their own schools. Their qualification to work as NLEs is explicitly stated in the selection criteria:

To be designated as an NLE rigorous criteria must be met. The most important of these being:
- the school's most recent Inspection will – other than in exceptional circumstances – have a judgement of outstanding overall, and outstanding for leadership and management
- contextual added value scores will exceed national averages
- the headteacher will have experience of supporting other schools
- the school will have the capacity to support others. (NCSL, 2007 page 2)

National leaders of education work in all of the ways described so far in this chapter. Their additional responsibilities of advising at national level and informing NCSL point to a new level of skills and strategies.

Implications for leadership

One of the problems with the models described in this chapter is that they have succeeded because of the work of remarkable people who happen to be school leaders. The extent to which their knowledge, personal qualities and professional practice can be transferred is a moot point. This issue is dealt with in detail in Chapter 8, but there are three specific aspects of leadership strategies that are particularly relevant to the context of this chapter: working as a consultant, a mentor or coach, or as facilitator (see Figure 5.1). Of course, these three strategies have much in common in that they are all professional helping strategies. As such they all share a cyclical approach to development or improvement – whether personal or organizational:

The components of each stage can be summarized as:

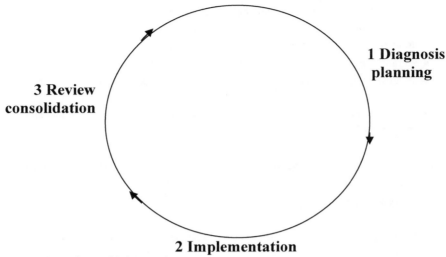

Figure 5.1 The professional helping cycle

1 Diagnosis and planning: analysis of the current situation, collection of evidence, identification of options, identification of the optimum way forward.

2 Implementation: taking action to change practice.

3 Review and consolidation: monitoring and reviewing strategies against needs, adjusting as necessary and then embedding them into sustainable and consistent practice.

In many ways the three strategies are a variation on a theme to find answers to the fundamental questions involved in any process of change:

- Where are we now and how do we know?
- Where do we need to be?
- What strategies and resources do we need to get there?
- What are our success criteria and how will we know if we have achieved them?
- What do we do next?

Consultants, mentors and coaches, and facilitators all use versions of this model in different guises. All helping relationships have to be based on agreed and explicit roles and relationships, as shown in Figure 5.2.

In working with schools systems, leaders have to identify the most appropriate stances for them to take in a given context – just 'being myself' may not be appropriate. Every helping relationship has to balance directive and non-directive approaches with regard to content (what has to be done) and process (how it will be done). For some schools, highly directive approaches on the improvement agenda

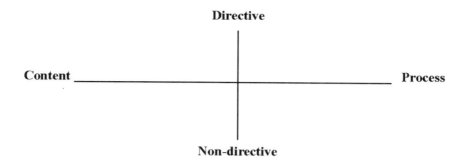

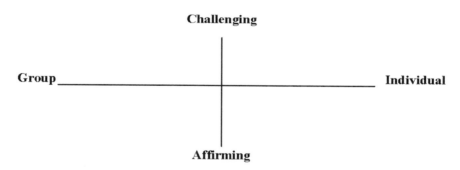

Figure 5.2 Roles and relationships in helping strategies

may be necessary but the culture of the school requires influence and persuasion rather than direction. In other circumstances the approaches may be reversed: the options available to a school are broad but individuals need to be directed to engage.

Helpers equally need to find the balance between challenge and affirmation and the extent to which that is individual or generic. Given the sensitivities involved in external agents coming into a school in difficulties, it is essential that the consultant, mentor/coach, facilitator gets the balance right and then acts consistently.

Consultancy

There are numerous definitions of consultancy, not all of them polite or professionally appropriate. In the context of system leadership, the following characteristics are probably appropriate to a consultant:

- usually an external change agent
- responds to a client's needs
- analyses the existing situation
- proposes relevant strategies.

Consultancy is most likely to be effective when the following criteria are met:

- There is an explicit, agreed and significant need to change.
- The relationship is based on mutual respect, trust and rapport.
- The contractual basis of the relationship is agreed at the outset.
- Timescales, outcomes and performance indicators are agreed.
- All strategies are based on evidence and rich data.
- The working culture is analytical, challenging and questioning.
- Information is presented according to the client's needs.
- The whole process is subject to regular review.

System leaders will not always work as consultants; often the contractual basis of their engagement will give them authority and accountability that are not appropriate to the consultancy role. However, system leaders will often have such a unique range of knowledge, skills and experiences that they will be seen as unique and special resources – too valuable to be ignored.

Mentoring and coaching

There is an almost theological debate about the difference between mentoring and coaching, and it is not the intention of this discussion to join that dispute. In this context mentoring may be defined as:

> A long-term, professional relationship, in which the mentor supports the learning, growth and development of the client.

By contrast coaching is:

> A short-term, focused and specific intervention to develop the skills, capability and confidence of the client in the technical aspects of their role.

There will, of course, be numerous gradations and permutations between these two positions. As in all aspects of system leaders' work, the important issue is appropriateness to context.

The *National Framework for Mentoring and Coaching* identifies ten principles:

- A learning conversation . . .
- Setting challenging and personal goals . . .
- A thoughtful relationship . . .
- Understanding why different approaches work . . .
- A learning agreement . . .
- Acknowledging the benefits to the mentors and coaches . . .
- Combining support from fellow professional learners and specialists . . .
- Experimenting and observing . . .
- Growing self-direction . . .
- Using resources effectively . . . (DfES, 2005d, page 13)

Facilitation

If consultancy is usually focused on organizational issues, and mentoring or coaching on the individual, then facilitation is concerned with helping teams and groups to learn and work effectively. Schwarz (2002) identifies the main task of the facilitator as:

> . . . **to help the group increase effectiveness by improving its process and structure.** *Process* refers to how a group works together. It includes how members talk to each other, how they identify and solve problems, how they make decisions, and how they handle conflict. *Structure* refers to stable recurring group process, examples being group membership or group roles. In contrast, *content* refers to what a group is working on. (page 5)

This definition is fundamental to the work of system leaders. It applies to every dimension of the role outlined on page 18. It is particularly relevant in:

- building capacity in their own schools
- learning to work with other schools, agencies and stakeholders
- working across communities
- developing capacity to work on policy formulation
- engaging with other system leaders.

Facilitation is perhaps best embodied in that it is the antithesis of positional power in meetings, where the chairman controls through setting the agenda, determining participation, defining outcomes and manipulating relationships – the classic transactional model. The effective negotiator, by contrast, works through:

- moral authority
- being inclusive and engaging, and valuing all members of the group

- being open and transparent
- being non-directive and evidence based
- building consensus and shared responsibility
- explicitly addressing process issues
- focusing on individual and group learning.

In conclusion, it is perhaps worth stressing a very obvious point. The skills, qualities and behaviours of system leaders working as consultants, mentors or coaches or as facilitators are those of effective school leaders. Equally, virtually all of them have a place in teams in schools and, most importantly, in the classroom. In many ways the roles and strategies described in this chapter are the primary source of developing capacity and sustainability in system leadership. Engagement in these strategies will build a cadre of school leaders who have the knowledge, skills, experience and, crucially, confidence to engage in leadership beyond the school.

6 Leading networks, clusters and federations

Just as extended services will affect every school leader's role, so involvement in networks, clusters and federations is likely to be equally pervasive and significant. Chapter 2 has already highlighted the central theme of system leadership – the move from independence and autonomy to interdependency and collaboration. This represents the greatest potential benefit to effective education but at the same time the most significant challenge to orthodox thinking about roles and relationships, structures and systems.

As discussed on page 13, there is a substantial body of theory relating to systems theory which again points to mutuality and interdependence as the most significant way forward for organizations:

> *The quantum organization must be flexible and responsive, at the edge.* Ambiguity, complexity, and rapid change increasingly dominate events both inside and outside the corporation ... Shifting boundaries of responsibility and identity, experimental modes of living and working, new information sources and new technological systems all demand flexible response. Mechanistic patterns of fixed functional or individual roles and rigidly organized structures for management and control inhibit the potential latent in human response, imagination, and organization. (Zohar, 1997, page 124)

Or Morrison (2002):

> A complex system comprises independent elements (which themselves might be made up of complex systems) which interact and give rise to organized behaviour in the system as a whole ... Order is not totally predetermined and fixed, but the universe (however defined) is creative, emergent (through iteration, learning and recursion), evolutionary and changing, transformative and turbulent. ... life is holistic and profoundly unpredictable. (page 9)

And:

> Complex adaptive systems possess a capability for self-organization which enables them to develop, extend, replace, adapt, reconstruct or change their internal structure (or *modus operandi*) so that they can respond to, and influence their environment. (page 14)

Rethinking the way organizations work points to a number of fundamental conceptual shifts:

- Ambiguity, complexity and change have become the norm.
- Our understanding of the world is shaped by new roles, responsibilities and relationships.
- The management of communication and information requires flexible strategies.
- Systems work through complex interactions and interdependency.
- Nothing is predictable, everything is emergent.
- Organizations have to be designed to be responsive.

In essence the future is networked, interdependent and emergent. The complexity of learning as a process and schools as organizations requires rethinking models of internal structures and external relationships. In practical terms this means increasing collaboration between schools with consequent changes in roles, relationships and accountability. This has profound implications for issues such as institutional identity, the nature of governance and our understanding of the nature of leadership.

This process is well established in the English education system and there is already a great deal of experience in moving towards different types of relationships. Three broad categories of relationship between schools were identified on page 20 – networks, clusters and federations.

Working in networks

A network was previously defined as an 'informal, voluntary association which is focused on a particular strategy or area of common interest'. Perhaps the best known and most widespread examples of networks in English education are the Networked Learning Communities established and developed by the NCSL between 2002 and 2006. These networks were highly significant both in what they achieved in terms of local outcomes but also in developing an understanding of what it means to work in networks – they developed a unique body of knowledge and expertise.

The basis of the NCSL Networked Learning Communities work can be summarized in terms of principles and processes:

Four principles of networked learning:
1 **Moral purpose** – a commitment to the success of all children.
2 **Shared leadership** – e.g. co-leadership and distributed leadership.
3 **Enquiry-based practice** – evidence and data-driven learning.
4 **Use of a model of learning** – systematic engagement with the 'three fields of knowledge'. (page 1)

Four processes of networked learning:
1. **Learning from one another** is where groups capitalize on their individual differences and diversity through sharing their knowledge, experience, expertise, practices and know-how.
2. **Learning with one another** is where individuals are doing the learning together, experiencing the learning together, co-constructing the learning, making meaning together. Collaborative practitioner enquiry or collaboratively learning about recent research are good examples of this activity.
3. **Learning on behalf of one another** is where the learning between individuals from different groups or schools is done on behalf of other individuals within their network – or wider system.
4. **Meta learning** is where individuals are additionally learning about the processes of their own learning so that they can replicate it in other situations or with other groups. (NCSL, 2006, page 1)

When networks work well, they have significant potential to enhance the quality of learning and teaching, as the following examples of Network Learning Community projects demonstrate:

- A multi-agency approach to improving learning with a specific focus on environmental factors and behaviour.
- The role of the student voice in learning.
- The strategic use of ICT to support independent learning.
- A 5–19 years writing project.
- 'Super learning days', when the normal curriculum is suspended.
- The development of interpersonal intelligence as a precursor to effective learning.
- 'Learning to learn' workshops for pupils and parents.

Irrespective of the chosen topic, working in networks has enormous potential:

... The leadership of organizations as natural systems wedded to modern networked communication patterns can help us work with rather than against the cultural diversity of our students, the professional diversity of our teachers, and the organizational diversity of our schools. Strong networked learning communities that have a compelling sense of purpose and work within clear parameters of collective, multiple, and light-touch forms of accountability, are one of the many strategies for restoring the rich diversity that years of standardization have depleted or destroyed. (Hargreaves and Fink, 2006, page 190)

The benefits of working in networks have been summarized by Ballantyne et al. (2006) as follows:

- Networks create conditions for complex relationships to work.
- Networks enable honest professional exchange.
- Networks provide a model for effective professional and leadership learning.
- Networks are hothouses for innovation.
- Networks build bridges between different agencies.
- Networks are a rich source of support.
- Networks offer unique opportunities for leadership development.
- Networks are loci for system transformation.

Such examples go a long way towards meeting Hargreaves' (2003) criteria for securing system wide transformation:

An effective lateral strategy for transferred innovation has several components, each of which tackles a strategic element that is currently neglected in government policy. It must become clear what is meant by 'good' and 'best' practice among teachers; there needs to be a method of locating good practices and sound innovations; innovations must be ones that bring real advantages to teachers, and methods of transferring innovation effectively have to be devised. (page 46)

The 'informality' and voluntary nature of networks is both their strength and their weakness – they work through mutual interest and advantage and are viable only to the extent that the advantage of membership transcends parochial issues. Loose coalitions only work to the extent to which membership and commitment are not in tension with self-interest. This is a classic manifestation of the movement from 'bonding' to 'bridging' described on page 77. Bridging enhances effectiveness and builds communities. For these reasons networks sometimes evolve into clusters.

Working in clusters

As defined above, a cluster is a 'more formal and structured relationship' than a network. The focus on learning as the unifying factor in Network Learning Communities is often replaced in clusters by operational and organizational integration, usually with a superordinate purpose:

- A voluntary cluster focused on CPD with shared in-service days, a pooled budget and the appointment of an administrator to facilitate effective and efficient use of resources and equitable access to provision.

- A local authority initiative where all schools become members of a geographical cluster with a board of management with the purpose of securing consistent and equitable access to effective learning.

- Clusters of primary schools working together to share expertise and resources to secure effective provision of extended services.

- Clusters that represent specific interests, e.g. faith schools, small primary schools or special schools.

- Cluster/consortium arrangements to ensure the delivery of the 14–19 curriculum; this involves collaboration between schools, FE colleges, employers, the Learning and Skills Council and the LA. In this context, the cluster enables integrated provision of the curriculum entitlement through deployment of staff, subject provision, liaison and coordination to ensure consistency.

- The movement towards the integration of the services in a number of schools which preserve the institutional autonomy, working practices, ethos and identity. Areas for integration could include:
  - Integrating of policies, e.g. behaviour and healthy eating.
  - Sharing staff expertise.
  - Joint clerical/administrative provision.
  - Shared cross-curricular themes.
  - Shared coordinator roles, e.g. special needs.
  - Shared provision and management of extended services.

- A cluster working as above but with a shared headteacher across the schools or with co-headship. This could well be paralleled by a combined governing body for the cluster with sub-committees responsible for each school.

The latter model is very close to a federation; indeed local usage might well describe it as a federation at the 'soft' end of the continuum. What is clear is that clusters bear a very strong resemblance to what Handy (1989) describes as federalism:

> Federalism implies a variety of individual groups allied together under a common
> flag with some shared identity. Federalism seeks to make it big by keeping it small,

or at least independent, by combining autonomy with co-operation. It is the method which businesses are slowly, and painfully, evolving for getting the best of both worlds – the size which gives them clout in the market-place and in the financial centres, as well as some economies of scale, and the small unit size which gives them the flexibility which they need, as well as the sense of community for which individuals increasingly hanker. (page 93)

Attractive clustering might be, there are situations where a totally new, more formal, organization is required – and this means a federation.

Working with federations

According to the Department for Education and Skills (DfES, 2005a):

> The term 'federation' has a wide currency, and is often used loosely to describe many different types of collaborative groups, partnerships and clusters, even through to mergers and the creation of new schools.
>
> For our purposes here, federations can be defined in two ways:
> - The definition as invoked in the 2002 Education Act which allows for the creation of a single governing body or a joint governing body committee across two or more schools from September 2003 onwards.
> - A group of schools with a formal (i.e. written) agreement to work together to raise standards, promote inclusion, find new ways of approaching teaching and learning and build capacity between schools in a coherent manner. This will be brought about in part through structural changes in leadership and management, in many instances through making use of the joint governance arrangements invoked in the 2002 Education Act. (page 1)

Hard federations 'sit at the hard end of a whole spectrum of collaborative arrangements' (DfES, 2005a, page 1). Within hard and soft federations, schools:

- retain their separate identity
- receive individual school budgets
- have separate Ofsted inspections
- report on performance individually.

A hard federation has a number of distinctive features:

- a single governing body
- common goals through a service-level agreement

- budgetary decisions can be made for all schools
- common leadership and management appointments can be made – including one headteacher for the group of schools.

Most of the above features are found at the Education Village, Darlington, i.e. a shared governing body and integrated leadership with a range of collaborative activities, e.g. CPD and curriculum innovation. Significantly, the governance and leadership of the federation is structured around the five outcomes of *Every Child Matters*.

There appears to be no consistency or consensus about the leadership and governance of federations:

> Consequently, leadership also varies across the Federations. Leadership may be exercised to varying degrees by the Executive Head/Director, the headteachers of constituent schools/colleges, governing bodies and their variants at school and/Federation level, or individual governors (particularly the chairs). To a large degree these represent structural differences, with different responsibilities, but there are also *ad hominem* variations. That is, those seen with very clear leadership roles, which are perceived as being carried out effectively, may include not only those with clear executive powers but also those whose role is apparently more facilitating. (Lindsay et al., 2005, page 6)

What is clear is that the leadership of federations is an emergent process with local history, politics and culture working in what is an essentially permissive statutory context. It would be naive to imagine that hard federations with common leadership and governance will not, over time, seek to become integrated institutions – especially on one-campus sites where the federation's identity will inevitably subsume the historical, separate identities.

Implications for leadership

A number of the issues relating to the successful leadership of networks, clusters and federations will be addressed in Chapter 7, in the context of the role of leaders building communities. The transition from being the leaders of a school (with all the cultural and historical baggage that implies) to leading a complex interaction of relationships is very challenging. In the philosopher Schopenhauer's parable, it is the dilemma of porcupines in winter – how to be together to keep warm yet avoid the pain of being too close to other porcupines. Any movement towards collaborative and integrated working faces issues of ego, territoriality, status and potential loss. Even in the most informal networks there will be micro-politics at play. This requires a rethink of the relevant leadership strategies and behaviours.

The specific implications of networks, clusters and federations for leadership behaviours and strategies would seem to be:

- securing consensus around common purpose and shared values
- developing systems and structures to ensure the effective functioning of the networks
- building trust and securing openness and transparency
- creating a sense of shared identity
- building capacity through shared learning and developing leadership capacity
- challenging poor or limited commitment and holding members of the network to account
- ensuring that resources are distributed equitably and managed efficiently
- creating a 'community of practice' so that learning is shared and the network understands its own learning process
- developing a commitment to monitoring, review and evaluation
- disseminating the learning of the network (in terms of outcomes and processes) to other networks.

The external evaluation of the NSCL Networked Learning Communities identifies a range of issues that has significant implications for the leadership of networks, clusters and federations. Earl et al. (2006) point to a number of 'key learnings':

1 Networked learning communities are complex, based in rich interactions of ideas and activities.
2 Networked learning communities influence pupil learning: engagement in a network is directly correlated with improvements in pupil performance.
3 The network is successful to the extent there is strong and pervasive engagement. The stronger the links and the more people that are involved, the greater the impact of the network.
4 Changing thinking and practice does occur as a result of engagement in a network but it is not found in every school in the network and reflects the levels of engagement and commitment in each institution.
5 However powerful the network, it is in schools that change actually occurs. The network enables, supports and encourages change – it does not produce change of itself.
6 Relationships and collaboration based in trust, shared understanding and collective responsibility are essential to the success of the network.
7 Joint work that challenges existing thinking and practices is a fundamental component of the potential contribution of involvement in networks.
8 Collaborative enquiry is the basis for significant change in practice and outcomes.
9 The success of a network is directly correlated with the clarity of its focus.

10 The traditional functions of leadership – vision and purpose, supporting development, monitoring and managing boundaries – remain significant.

11 Leadership is distributed across the network.

In summary:

> Networked learning communities are made up of complex interactions between structures and activities. Each of the features has a role to play, and like any complex system, the ways in which they combine and interact are innumerable and cannot be predicted in any particular context. Any change in any one invites changes in the others. (Earl et al., 2006, page 14)

The movement to system leadership, especially in the context of networks, clusters and federations, requires a fundamental rethink of how leaders work. One of the legacies of the school improvement policies of the 1990s in England has been the introduction of a quasi-market approach based on competition between schools for students. This approach is based on the myth of perfect competition – parents do not have equal access and genuine choice. All forms of collaboration are potentially compromised by the need to ensure the viability of individual schools. This situation is exacerbated in some areas by falling rolls.

If collaboration between schools is to really work then, in time, the pattern of accountability will have to change as will the culture based on institutional autonomy. A significant alternative perspective might be found in the concept of Wikinomics. The basis of Wikinomics is a wiki – computer software that allows users to create and edit web pages (hence Wikipedia). Wiki comes from a Hawaiian word for fast.

The key premise of Wikinomics is collaboration:

> . . . The new promise of collaboration is that with peer production we will harness human skill, ingenuity, and intelligence more efficiently and effectively than anything we have witnessed previously. Sounds like a tall order. But the collective knowledge, capability, and resources embodied within broad horizontal networks of participants can be mobilized to accomplish much more than one firm acting alone. Whether designing an airplane, assembling a motorcycle, or analyzing the human genome, the ability to integrate the talents of dispersed individuals and organizations is become *the* defining competency for managers and firms. (Tapscott and Williams, 2006, page 18)

Tapscott and Williams (2006) identify four principles of Wikinomics:

Being open: this involves 'candour, transparency, freedom, flexibility, expansiveness, engagement and access' (page 21). In essence this is about transparency and sharing; maximizing the transfer of ideas and innovation.

Peering: Wikinomics is non-hierarchical; it invites involvement and collaboration and is based on self-organization rather than hierarchical control models. Peering encourages participations from any source.

Sharing: in essence involves the end of copyright and patents, thus allowing for shared improvement and the development of ideas, projects and strategies.

Acting globally: means moving beyond the parochial and interacting with a far larger community than ever before. The economic growth of India and China, the collapse of communism and the Human Genome Project are all the result of global interaction.

This might all seem very utopian, but Tapscott and Williams start with the story of a gold mining company in economic difficulties that broke the fundamental taboo of the industry by publishing all its geological data on the internet and asking for advice on where to mine for gold – and offering a reward. The turnover of the company increased from $100 million to $9 billion – almost entirely because of openness, collaboration and a willingness to challenge authority.

Wikinomics is almost entirely based on the internet – but what else is the internet but networks, clusters and federations? This means that leadership has to be morally, culturally and practically involved in bridging, in creating interdependence and focusing on the 'sum' rather than 'the parts'.

7 Educational leadership and the community

This chapter explores the relationship between school leaders and the community that their school serves. Headteachers have always had a symbolic role in their communities, representing one of the most significant elements in the success of any area. However, the precise nature of that role has changed significantly over the years. Equally, the nature of the community that a school serves is highly diffuse, ranging from the very tight geographical areas that most primary schools serve, to the much more diffuse context of many secondary schools, to the complex and multi-layered provision of special schools. What has been consistent is the professional focus on the school itself as the centre of the school leaders' work. This is reinforced by contractual arrangements and models of accountability.

The Audit Commission report (2006), *More than the Sum*, makes a compelling case for increasing the interaction between schools and the wider community:

> Traditional school improvement activity has tended to concentrate on teaching and learning at individual school level. Critical though this is, by itself the approach is limited . . . (page 3)

> The strong relationship between parental socio-economic circumstances and children's attainment is longstanding, and clear at both school and pupil level. (page 4)

> Children's educational underachievement is linked with a wide range of deprivation factors: low parental qualifications, poor housing conditions, low family income, ill-health, family problems and wider community factors such as low aspirations and unemployment. (page 4)

This leads to a clear and unequivocal conclusion for the Audit Commission (2006):

> Because of this, improving schools and improving the prospects of the most disadvantaged pupils in schools is not a matter for schools alone or for schools supported only by external education professionals. (page 6)

> School improvement and renewal are inseparable issues from neighbourhood improvement and renewal, particularly in the most disadvantaged areas. While schools are profoundly affected by their neighbourhoods, they equally have a key role in promoting cohesion and building social capital . . . (page 6)

The final proposition by the Audit Commission represents a fundamental challenge to prevailing orthodoxy and calls into question many of the basic assumptions that have informed discussions about the nature of leadership effectiveness.

This view is reinforced by Her Majesty's Chief Inspector in her Annual Report (2007) where she draws a direct correlation between poverty and academic performance:

> But the challenge remains. How do we reduce the gap in opportunities and outcomes between the majority of children and young people and those who continue to lag behind? The relationship between poverty and outcomes for young people is stark; the poor performance of many children and young people living in the most disadvantaged areas is seen in the Foundation Stage Early Learning Goals, in National Curriculum test results, and in GCSE results. (page 6)
>
> Recent data analyses and research studies confirm the close association between poverty and low educational achievement, with pupils from low income backgrounds continuing to perform less well than more advantaged pupils. (page 65)
>
> - At Key Stage 2, in 2006, 61% of pupils eligible for free school meals achieved the expected level in English and 58% achieved it in mathematics. This compares with 83% and 79% respectively of those pupils not eligible.
> - In the GCSE examinations in 2006, the proportion of pupils gaining five or more A*–C grades was 33% among those eligible for free school meals. The figure for the non-eligible group was 61%. (page 65)

These two, highly authoritative perspectives represent a significant shift in thinking at national policy level. For many years it was argued that schools could improve, in spite of the environment they served. What is now emerging is recognition that a focus on the school alone is not sufficient to achieve equity and maximize life chances for every child and young person. This has profound implications for the traditional role of school leader and may be seen as a key motivation for system leadership.

Her Majesty's Chief Inspector points to the direct causal relationship between poverty and underachievement. It may be significant that the UNICEF report (2007), *Child poverty in perspective*, found that child well-being was highest in those countries with relatively low levels of child poverty. There seems to be very little that school leaders can do at local level to alleviate the worst effects of child poverty – that is an issue for national strategies and, more importantly, a national culture that finds the notion of children living in poverty abhorrent.

One of the factors that can serve to remediate the worst effects of poverty is social capital. The Audit Commission (2006) stresses the importance of social capital in terms of life chances and well-being. It may be that social capital – the quality of life in the community – offers the greatest leverage and most significant potential for impact for school leaders. Apart from the school itself, it is the area that offers the greatest potential for significantly influencing children and young people's life chances, well-being, educational achievement and happiness.

The variables influencing life chances

In broad terms, it is possible to identify four variables that will determine the success or failure (however defined) of a child or young person. These may be defined as: a) physical factors; b) social factors; c) personal factors; and d) school factors.

The first category reflects our genetic inheritance – factors such as gender, race and disability. These cannot, of themselves, be changed – although attitudes towards them can. Educational leaders have done much to mitigate the potentially negative effects of these variables, although there is no doubt that, in many societies, being a woman or disabled, or belonging to a minority ethnic group, can seriously compromise life chances. The issue, therefore, is to create an understanding that difference is not the issue; it is how that difference is responded to and managed that is crucial.

The social factors refer to such variables as poverty, family, social class and social capital/community. Social class in Britain confers significant advantage and remains a significant determinant of life chances. It is an aspect of education that may have been ameliorated in recent years but remains a key factor. Poverty is equally stubborn in its abiding impact on human potential. The family is hugely significant especially in the primary years.

> . . . a great deal of the variation in students' achievement is outside the school's influence. Family social class, for example, accounts for about one third of such variance. (Desforges, 2003, page 21)
>
> . . . parental involvement in the form of 'at-home' interest and support is a major force in shaping pupils' educational outcomes. (page 22)
>
> The higher the social class the more parental involvement is evident. (page 21)

Social capital, of all the social factors, is the most amenable to intervention strategies.

The personal factors are the qualities and characteristics that the individual learner brings into the education system, and will include such elements as personal motivation and aspiration, readiness to learn, personal resilience and sustainability, ability and intelligence. The movement towards personalizing learning is an explicit recognition of the need to engage with the individual on his or her own terms. *Every Child Matters* is also recognition of the need to focus on the entitlement of every child and young person.

As the Audit Commission recognized, the school has been the primary focus of government policy for the well-being of children and young people for many years – yet it is the factor most influenced by the other three.

> Most school effectiveness studies show that 80% or more of student achievement can be explained by student background rather than schools. (Silins and Mulford, 2002, page 561)

This view is reinforced by Leithwood et al. (2007):

> While leadership explains only five to seven per cent of the difference in pupil learning and achievement across schools (not to be confused with the typically very large differences among pupils within schools), this difference is actually about one-quarter of the total difference across schools (12 to 20 per cent) explained by all school-level variables, after controlling for pupil intake or background factors. (page 4)

This is not to minimize what an effective school can do:

> Analysis of a sample of inspection reports for outstanding schools in areas of economic deprivation revealed that these schools had a number of features in common. Responsibilities were shared among a strong team of senior staff, so that the success of the school did not depend wholly upon the leadership of the headteacher, as important as that was. Staff were ambitious in their expectations of the pupils' achievement. They provided high quality teaching, made careful use of assessment and provided close support for individual pupils' personal and academic development. These schools provided a broad and rich curriculum, with a clear focus on raising attainment in the basic skills of literacy and numeracy. Pupils entered with standards below those found nationally and made outstanding progress, often leaving with attainment in line with or even above the national average. (HMCI, 2007, page 65)

However, if Silins and Mulford's view is accepted then there are two pivotal conclusions:

1 It is essential that the 20 per cent of the variables represented by the school is as effective as possible.

2 If the school is to influence life chances, well-being and the outcomes of *Every Child Matters*, then it will have to move into the 80 per cent.

As has been argued above, of the three variables that make up the 80 per cent, the social factors are increasingly being recognized and the social factor that is most likely to pay dividends is the area of social capital.

Social capital, community and schools

All successful school leaders understand social capital – their ability to develop their school as a community is one of the most significant explanations of their success. The challenge for system leaders is the extent to which they are able, conceptually and practically, to extend and apply the strategies and skills that they have developed within the school to the wider community.

Sergiovanni (2005) is explicit about the benefits of a community focus to a school:

- Community helps satisfy the need that teachers, students, and parents have to be connected to each other and to the school.
- Community helps everyone in the school to focus on the common good.
- Community provides students with a safe harbour in a stormy sea – a place where they are accepted unconditionally.
- Community supports learning.
- Community builds relationships and responsibility.
- Community connects people to their work for moral reasons that obligate them to respond. (page 56)

Each of these six elements can be extended (without much modification) to the community that the school serves and to the other communities that it engages with. The importance of focusing on the school *and* the wider community is stressed by Bryk and Schneider (2002, pages 138–139):

> Moreover, the tendency in policy discussions today to emphasize the need for instructional improvement can work to silence discussion about addressing equally important relational needs. To be clear, this is not an either-or situation in our view. Instructional improvement is very much needed in urban school communities. Strengthening the social base for engaging students, teachers, and parents around more ambitious learning, however, also is essential. (page 138)

Thus, our research suggests that effective urban schools need teachers that not only know their students well, but also have an empathetic understanding of their parents' situations and have the interpersonal skills needed to engage these adults effectively. (page 139)

The tension between the focus on the school and the focus on the wider community might be seen in terms of the difference between Gemeinschaft and Gesellschaft – where the former focuses on the individual, subordinating self-interest to a higher social unity, and the latter describes a situation where self-interest dominates. The movement from Gesellschaft to Gemeinschaft can be seen as emblematic of the movement from leadership of the individual institution to system leadership.

Social capital is an elusive and contested topic but most of us will recognize its components as the basis for explaining the quality of our working and professional lives. The following classification of the components of social capital, i.e. the criteria for an effective community, is defined by West-Burnham et al. (2007):

- Shared social norms and values: a clear consensus about the moral basis of the community, principles are known, shared, understood and acted on – they inform community and personal decisions.
- Sophisticated social networks: clear and rich lines of communication with shared language, a common vocabulary and high quality dialogue.
- High levels of trust: openness, consistency and reliability.
- High civic engagement: people are good citizens; they vote, stand for election and participate in the civic community.
- Symbols and rituals: the community has a sense of identity that is celebrated through shared ceremonies and events.
- Interdependence and reciprocity: there is a high level of caring and sharing, people 'look out for each other'.
- Volunteering and community action: people join in; create clubs, societies and charities, and feature prominently in community action. (page 32)

To this original list might be added:

- Shared hope and aspiration: a sense of common purpose and optimism about the future of the community.
- Learning and wisdom: the community enables effective learning and grows through learning and shares wisdom.

Any successful school – as with any successful social enterprise – will be able to provide examples of its success in achieving each of these criteria. When a significant proportion is present, then the development of a community can become exponential as each element reinforces and extends the others. If, as the Audit Commission implies, school leaders need to engage with social capital beyond the school, then the traditional model of effective leadership behaviours has to be extended to engagement with the community in all its forms.

Table 7.1 Social capital and leadership behaviour

Component of social capital	Leadership behaviours
1 Values and norms	Moral leadership; modelling behaviours; protocols, consistency, vision
2 Social networks	Shared language; common vocabulary; dialogue
3 Trust	Consistency; openness; emotional intelligence; credibility
4 Civic engagement	Securing participation; distributed leadership. Works through influence
5 Symbols and rituals	Building shared identity; celebrating the community
6 Interdependence	Caring; building empathy; building leadership capacity; inclusive
7 Volunteering	Shared commitment; altruism, encourages collaboration
8 Hope	Optimistic perspective and language; strategic thinking; scenario building
9 Learning	Modelling effective learning; enabling learning

In Putnam's (2000) terms, social capital is developed through bonding – building capacity within the community. System leadership implies going beyond bonding to bridging – building social capital between communities.

Diamond (2005) tells the sad story of the demise of the Norse society in Greenland in the fourteenth century:

> Five adjectives, mutually somewhat contradictory, characterize Greenland Norse society: communal, violent, hierarchical, conservative and euro-centric. (page 235)

The net result of these factors explains the collapse of a sophisticated, educated and, at one time, economically successful community. It was unable to change, to adapt and to get on with its neighbours (the Inuit). In effect it was so focused on bonding that it was unable to bridge. The Norse settlers lived, and died, as Euro-peans, perpetuating inappropriate cultural, social and economic norms and practices. Paradoxically their need to retain a sense of community led to their downfall – because of their failure to learn, to engage and create a new identity relevant to changing circumstances. Without resorting to the melodramatic, the future success of schools may be contingent on their ability to bridge. As with the Norse settlers, it is the leadership of schools that will determine the desire and capacity to move from bonding to bridging.

Education leadership and the community

There can never be a blueprint for the extent to which, and how, school leaders engage with the community beyond the school – context is everything. Interventions that are entirely appropriate in one community will be entirely counter-productive in another. In most respects the level of engagement will be determined by the extent to which the social variables discussed above are positive or negative. The more negative they are the more intervention may be justified. Figure 7.1 shows the range of leadership responses that are possible – which one is right will be determined by time and context.

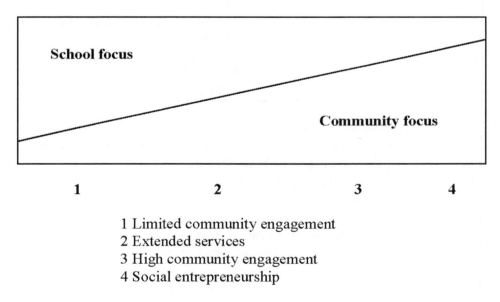

1 Limited community engagement
2 Extended services
3 High community engagement
4 Social entrepreneurship

Figure 7.1 The scope of leadership engagement with the community

School leaders, headteachers in particular, will always have some degree of formal engagement with schools, equally they will always have some interaction with the wider community – there are no absolutes. System leadership is all about finding the appropriate place on the continuum that is right for the school and possible for the individual. The specific characteristics of each stage can be defined as follows:

1 Limited community engagement: this is the historical pattern that predominated until recent years with a few distinguished exceptions. Leadership is primarily focused on the school as an autonomous institution with the majority of leadership time and energy being focused on the internal efficiency and effectiveness of the school. In this context, headship is primarily concerned with the integrity of the school – this model is reinforced by current patterns of accountability and a substantial majority of the National Standards for Headteachers.

   For most purposes, community is defined as parents, with some engagement with other schools and perhaps local businesses. In many ways the school is essentially passive as far as the issues identified in the first part of this chapter are concerned. There is no tradition of active intervention in the variables that determine the effectiveness of the school – possibly, and understandably, because the school is highly successful by a range of criteria.

   A school that is in difficulties might also be in this position – simply because it has to focus all its energies on getting the 20 per cent right. This is again justifiable and is manifest in the strategies discussed in Chapter 4.

   Historically, many schools claimed a distinctive community ethos but, in the context of this chapter, this actually meant that a limited range of school resources were available for community usage, *on the school's terms*. Then, as now, school leadership was largely focused on bonding: building the internal capacity of the school.

2 Extended services: this aspect of school leadership has been dealt with in depth in Chapter 3. It represents the emerging model of school leadership and one that will largely supplant the historic approach described above. In summary, the most significant implications for school leaders would seem to be:
   - A changing pattern of accountability focusing on the outcomes of *Every Child Matters* and well-being.
   - The duty to collaborate with all of the agencies providing services to children and young people.
   - A new relationship with parents, with them becoming potentially more engaged through Parent Councils.
   - Extended and more diverse usage of the school's resources.
   - Increasing collaboration with other schools.

3 High community engagement: this stage represents a significant departure from the historic norms of headship. It is the position where engagement with the social variables described above becomes a fundamentally significant component of a school leader's role. This is still working from a school perspective, i.e. the involvement is based in the school and is primarily designed to support the pupils of the school. However, it means engaging in a range of activities that are not found in any headteacher's contract, the National Standards for Headteachers or normal expectations of the role of school leader.

   An example of this approach in practice is Ashbrow Infant School, Kirklees:

Inspired by the headteacher's leadership and vision, there is a very strong belief held by staff in this infant school that the school is both a community and a family resource and that the school has a critical role in trying to break cycles of deprivation and raise aspirations. Many parents have had bad experiences of school and need to change their view so those attitudes are not passed on to the children. Under an enterprising headteacher, the school places an emphasis on numerous small initiatives, not one of which is necessarily making the big difference but all contributing to the philosophy of community engagement in action.

Examples of activities/initiatives include

- a 'forest school' which facilitates outdoor education on site;
- a children's centre;
- adult classes;
- access to social services on site through a family support worker, which improves accessibility and avoids the stigma of being referred;
- free legal advice on site through a local solicitor;
- play schemes, where parents, rather than dropping children off, join in too as a family; and
- using lunchtimes for social skills – food is served by an adult at the table as in family groups. Parents regularly come in to have lunch with children and take on this role. (Audit Commission, 2006, page 19)

All of these projects can be seen as having a direct impact on every aspect of a child's education but they all recognize the totality of a child's life – i.e. a holistic view going beyond the boundaries of the school.

4 Social entrepreneurship: this category moves the debate into relatively uncharted territory. In the most abstract and theoretical sense, leadership, as social entrepreneurship, moves the role of school leader from reproduction (systems maintenance) to systems transformation:

Schools . . . are sites where the intellectual activity taking place in them is inextricably linked to broader social and cultural concerns. For example, curriculum content, special education, and other class placement based on race, class, gender, and disability may reflect society's discriminatory perceptions and practices. The moral nature of transformative leadership, unlike traditional notions of school administration, not only locates the work of schools in a broader social context, but argues that students should become accountable as well as responsible for their own education. (Dantley and Tillman, 2006, page 21)

In this context, the role of the school leaders is restorative rather than palliative – moving from a 'find and fix' mentality of putting things right to a 'predict and prevent' approach, seeking to stop things going wrong. The emphasis moves away from activities that are directly relevant to the school, to those that only have indirect and long-term benefits. In most cases they will involve leadership in the community that may not grow directly out of the role of the school leader. The distinction between the professional role and personal morality may thus be blurred. Hypothetical examples of such activities could include:

- Involvement in a local campaign on environmental issues, e.g. industrial pollution affecting children's health.

- Joining a partnership focusing on gang violence, drug related crime and gun crime.
- Initiating projects to create employment opportunities.
- Becoming involved in projects related to effective families and domestic violence.

There can never be an expectation that school leaders would automatically become involved in such activities. Many do, of course, but as a matter of personal conscience rather than contractual obligation. This raises the issue of educational leadership as having a significant role to play in the achievement of social justice in society. This highlights profound moral, cultural and professional questions and returns to the issues raised in Chapter 2 – where are the boundaries of leadership? Running a good school will always be fundamental to headship, how to achieve a good school is open to new and potentially radical interpretations. Rather in the way that the Church is expected to stay out of politics, there will be those who argue that the role of school leaders is to be in schools.

However, as the issues identified at the start of the chapter becomes more central to our understanding of the nature of effective education, then there may be an increasing recognition of the importance of this dimension of system leadership.

8

The knowledge, qualities and behaviours of system leaders

System leadership does not compromise or supersede what we know about effective school leadership in general or headship in particular. As has been frequently argued, it rather requires existing models of effective leadership to be extended and new strategies to be developed. There is now a substantial consensus as to the essential components of school leadership. PricewaterhouseCoopers (2007) summarize these as:

- strategic direction and ethos
- teaching and learning
- developing and managing people
- networking and collaboration
- operations
- accountability.

All of these are relevant to the system leader, although there are clear issues in translating them to different contexts and working on a different model of authority and accountability. However, it would be naive to assume that all headteachers will be able to transfer from school to system leadership with confidence. Pricewater-houseCoopers (2007) identify three major areas of concern:

> . . . However, there was also a sense in which the data suggested some school leaders were more comfortable with an operational role rather than a strategic one. (page 5)

> . . . when headteachers were asked what their priorities should be when going forward, as well as what their future skills needs were, staff management, recruitment and retention appeared quite far down the list. Whilst this is under-standable given their other commitments, it nevertheless suggests that many school

leaders may not have embraced the people agenda as fully as has been the case in other sectors . . . (page 5)

. . . school leaders now have to be much more outward looking than they used to be, and this has clear implications around the need for a range of 'softer' inter-personal skills around networking and communication. Our research shows that most school leaders recognise and accept the new requirements being placed on them in these areas, but that many are struggling to respond, and most recognise the need for training and support. (page 6)

It would be wrong to attribute too much significance to these findings but, given the distinctive characteristics of system leadership, they do raise potential areas for concern. There is, quite understandably and properly, very limited understanding of the attributes of system leaders and certainly no clear consensus exists as yet.

In 2004–2005, NCSL and the Innovations Unit of the DfES funded a programme focusing on leadership beyond the school. All the participants were 'excellent' or 'outstanding' heads and all were involved in many of the manifestations of system leadership described in this book so far. As a final exercise they were asked to develop a national standard for system leaders using the National Standards for Headteachers as a model. Their final version is reproduced below:

Towards a National Standard for System Leadership
Notes from Executive Leadership Programme pilot group, 2005
System leadership

> System leaders have a responsibility to inspire and cultivate leadership beyond their immediate community. This implies challenging current practice and inspiring lead learners and other stakeholders to create a culture of change to ensure that 'Every child matters' and to raise standards at local and national level.
> They have the responsibility to create networks, clusters and federations that will help to secure equity and excellence across the system. They will facilitate credible and informed professional input into the wider system – i.e. the political, social, economic infrastructure. They will articulate, co-construct and influence specific agendas, policies and strategies around raising educational achievement.

Knowledge:
System leaders will know about:

- a range of leadership models that will impact on system change
- strategies which bring about system transformation, change and improvement
- how culture and context influence system leadership
- the complexities of the system and the policy making process
- the organic nature of complex organisations, clusters, networks and federations
- the global perspective and the local, national, international trends and their impact on schools and education generally
- the current political, social, economic infrastructure and education's place within it.

Professional qualities

System leaders will demonstrate:

- commitment to leadership in a wider context
- commitment to developing local, national and international policy
- commitment to raising standards across the system
- the ability to engage in constructive dialogue with policy makers
- the ability to continually re-shape and articulate a vision
- confidence in developing evidence based strategies for change
- confidence in challenging current thinking and orthodoxy
- understanding of the concept of moral leadership and its relationship with whole system responsibility
- sustained enthusiasm and energy in complex and challenging circumstances
- understanding of the need for critical and reflective thinking and sustained personal learning and development.
- the interpersonal skills needed to influence and facilitate change, communication and connectivity.

Actions

System leaders will work to:

- promote an understanding of system level leadership at local and national level
- seek ways of influencing policy and decision making at all levels
- work collaboratively with all stakeholders to bring about system change
- change the working environment to reflect new ways of learning and leading
- ensure professional growth for all in the system
- collaborate with others to build leadership capacity
- work effectively to support and encourage teams to develop and challenge their vision
- work across the infrastructure to develop integrated approaches
- identify the need for system change or new systems and drive change forward
- engage in futures thinking
- analyse the impact of change on the system
- collaborate and develop others beyond their own environment
- manage projects to successful completion
- monitor, review and evaluate to demonstrate impact.

From this detailed overview it is possible to identify a number of broad principles that should inform any discussion of the nature and components of system leadership.

These principles can be best expressed by focusing on three dimensions of leadership:

- The knowledge base that is necessary to be able to work effectively.
- The qualities that inform personal engagement, credibility and sustainability.

- The behaviours that translate principle into practice.

> . . . Leader formation programs should be carefully constructed to ensure that they assist participants to further develop and refine the culture of their intellects. Such programs should adopt an interdisciplinary approach to expand participants' horizons and to enable them to better appreciate that intelligence is holistic, connecting them to the universe of knowledge and to their wholeness as human beings. (Duignan, 2006, page146)

Knowledge

There is no doubt that the bedrock of system leadership is detailed understanding, based in successful personal experience, of the strategies that lead to school improvement, effectiveness and high performance. Crucially, system leaders will need to be able to rationalize and explain their success, and adapt and apply it to other contexts.

The knowledge base of system leaders will also need to include, in no particular order of priority, awareness and understanding of:

- examples of innovation and best practice from schools across the system
- the national and international trends that are likely to inform policy development
- the portfolio of leadership strategies that will impact on system change, improvement and transformation
- the statutory, structural and cultural factors influencing systems working at institutional, local and national level
- educational research and data to inform their personal understanding and confidence.

All of this implies that system leaders truly understand the system in which they work as a whole:

> The new breakthroughs are complex and sophisticated, and will require leaders who have more comprehensive conceptualization than most leaders have at the present (more accurately, systems have not fostered and permitted the development of such leadership). The new knowledge, as I have said, is being led not by academic theoreticians; the new theoreticians are certain policymakers and lead practitioners working with a wider set of ideas and interacting with academics, who themselves are immersed in practical theorizing and doing. This is crucial because it means the ideas and strategies are being formed around real problems – big ones never before solved. (Fullan, 2005, page xii)

Qualities

Knowledge and expertise alone can never be the basis of effective leadership. System leaders face unique challenges that can only be met by being able to draw on a rich portfolio of personal characteristics or qualities. Duignan (2006) discusses the idea of the capable leader:

> . . . I am defining capable people as those who engage with the ethical and moral dimensions of life as well as the cognitive, factual and rationals. They go beyond the competent person's rational analyses of facts and situations, and develop a 'wisdom way of knowing'. (page 122)

> . . . Wisdom is often equated with 'intuition' or with having a 'gut feeling' about something or someone. In the argument presented here, 'gut feeling' encompasses the wisdom derived from experiences of life. It embraces the cognitive and practical as well as the emotive and spiritual dimensions of life, wrapping the cognitive and practical in wise emotive and spiritual frames to take a fully human view of the situation. (pages 122–123)

In the context of system leadership, where situational power will rarely be an option, there seem to be two dominant qualities that are most likely to give full expression to the sort of wisdom that Duignan describes: influence and storytelling. In his discussion of leaders who were highly successful in leading complex and diverse populations, Gardner (2004) argues:

> . . . They did not just tell a simple, familiar story more effectively. Rather, they took on a far more daunting task: to develop a new story, tell it well, embody it in their lives, and help others understand why it deserves to triumph over the simpler counterstory. Moreover, they drew continually and imaginatively on several other levers of mind change: reason, multiple modes of representation, and resonance with the experiences of those whom they sought to influence. (pages 88–89)

Perkins (2003) identifies a parallel and equally powerful strategy:

> . . . communities, organizations and human collectives of all sorts are 'made of conversations,' if we mean conversations in the general sense of interactions. Metaphorically, conversations are the virtual neurons that bind individuals into a larger-scale cognitive collective. Conversations can be progressive (good knowledge processing, positive symbolic conduct) or regressive (poor knowledge processing, negative symbolic conduct). (page 37)

Integrating these two perspectives points to leaders who are more than effective communicators but are rather able to communicate a compelling sense of the future, secure engagement and commitment to that vision and create shared understanding that informs practice. This requires much more than a set of technical skills – rather a set of personal qualities. In this context, qualities are defined as authentic and deeply ingrained approaches to human engagement.

Clarity of purpose

Moral purpose is a common denominator in almost any discussion of any form of leadership. In system leadership it becomes even more significant as the complexity of the role increases and the traditional reference points are less secure. It could be argued, for example, that in the final analysis the only moral rationale for system leadership is to secure excellence and equity across the system. The focus on equity points to an explicit commitment to social justice. Indeed, as was argued in Chapter 1, the primary rationale for system leadership is to address the systematic problems in the provision of education in England:

> As the main institution for fostering social cohesion in an increasingly diverse society, publicly funded schools must serve all children, not simply those with the loudest and most powerful advocates. This means addressing the cognitive and social needs of all children, with an emphasis on including those who may not have been well served in the past ... addressing what in England has been termed 'the long tail of under-achievement.' (Fullan, 2003, page 3)

The moral dimensions of system leadership might be summarized as:

- A passionate commitment to social justice, equity and inclusion.
- A focus on the entitlement of the individual.
- Openness and transparency in all working.
- Behaviours and strategies that are concrete expressions of the principles of *Every Child Matters*, well-being and community cohesion.

Comfort with complexity and ambiguity

This includes the ability to work in a context without clear boundaries and parameters, with uncertain outcomes and where roles and status are unclear. One of the characteristics of an effective school is its predictability, linearity and consistency. The school timetable is the classic exemplification of this. System leadership lacks the potential for control and certainty. System leaders will therefore need to:

... set aside all consideration of existing conditions, free themselves to think in accordance with their deepest beliefs, and do not bind their thinking with structure and practices before considering meaning and values, they usually discover that the number and variety of people and entities to participate in governance, ownership, rewards, rights, and obligations are much greater than anticipated. They usually find their deepest beliefs require transcendence of existing institutional boundaries and practices. (Hock, 1999, pages 9–10)

System leaders get their confidence and security from deep beliefs – not structures and procedures.

The ability to influence, advise and negotiate

Working beyond the school involves using different types of authority – switching from positional to political. Working with policy-makers, other agencies and other headteachers requires a portfolio of strategies rooted in personal credibility and sophisticated interpersonal strategies:

> ... Achieving constructive influence involves expressing ourselves in a way that produces a desired social result, like putting someone at ease. Artfully expressive people are viewed by others as confident and likeable and in general make favorable impressions. (Goleman, 2006, page 95)

> Deciding on the optimal dose of expressivity depends, among other factors, on social cognition, knowing the governing cultural norms for what's appropriate in a given social context ... (page 96)

Influencing, advising and negotiating imply the deployment of a range of inter-personal skills and a fundamental commitment to 'win-win' transactions. Working in classrooms and schools may not always be the best preparation for such approaches.

Building networks and coalitions

The absence of the formal structures of school requires skills in developing sophis-ticated networks to support and extend influence, communications and sharing information, and the development of coalitions to pursue policies and inform the development of policy. This topic has already been explained in depth in Chapter 6. In summary, it is worth stressing that system leaders have the characteristics of what Gladwell (2000) calls connectors: people who

- have large personal and professional networks; they know a lot of people in different contexts
- enjoy social engagement, building networks and social relationships
- cultivate and affirm relationships that are open and available

- are personally credible and valued by others
- make connections between people and ideas.

Developing communities of practice

If system leadership is to be effective and sustainable, then those engaged in it will have to be deliberate and systematic in developing their own and shared learning as they develop experience and expertise. This implies that system leaders are very conscious of their own learning, collaborate in supporting each other's learning and ensure that their joint learning is shared and made public. System leaders will have to see the development of communities of practice as an intrinsic element of their role. Wenger (1998) summarizes their importance as:

- *Negotiation of meaning.* In communities of practice, participation and reification are deeply interwoven into a sustained history of practice, . . .
- *Preservation and creation of knowledge.* Because communities of practice are sustained by the negotiation of meaning, they can be attuned to emerging needs and opportunities . . .
- *Spreading of information.* The mutual accountability derived from pursuing a joint enterprise and the interpersonal relations built over time together make the sharing of information necessary, relevant and tailored . . .
- *Home for identities.* A focus on communities of practice does not entail paying less attention to individuals. On the contrary, it places a very specific focus on people, . . . (pages 251–252)

Facilitating dialogue

Dialogue is fundamental to the characteristics identified so far. The ability to engage in dialogue is fundamental to any complex social process involving reconciling perceptions, building consensus and securing agreement. This involves multiple, rich and effective conversations across the system. Given what has been discussed so far about the work of system leaders, it is clear that dialogue is central to their work. It would be wrong to think of dialogue as sophisticated communication skills – it is much more an expression of values and an attitude. The essential characteristics of effective dialogue can be summarized as:

- parity of esteem for people and their beliefs and ideas
- securing clarity of purpose and outcomes
- making reasoning and assumptions explicit
- testing understanding and conclusions
- accepting uncertainty and ambiguity

- building and developing ideas
- encouraging and providing feedback
- questioning and challenging
- reviewing process and outcomes.

> In a dialogue, however, nobody is trying to win. Everybody wins if anybody wins. There is a different sort of spirit to it. In a dialogue, there is no attempt to gain points, or to make your particular view prevail. Rather, whenever any mistake is discovered on the part of anybody, everybody gains. It's a situation called win-win ... (Bohm, 1996, page 7)

> Dialogue is really aimed at going into the whole thought process and changing the way the thought process occurs collectively. We haven't really paid much attention to thought as a process. We have *engaged* in thoughts, but we have only paid attention to the content, not to the process. (page 10)

Building leadership capacity

Most system leaders will probably remain headteachers – this means that they will need to build leadership capacity in their own schools to 'cover' their absence. There is also a need to develop understanding of the nature of system leadership itself. This means that system leaders will be very good at distributing leadership. They will see leadership as collective capacity rather than personal status and use every opportunity to develop leadership capacity in others. Distributed leadership implies:

- Ensuring that authority and responsibility are balanced.
- Decision making is located at the appropriate point.
- Leadership development is available for all.
- Teams have genuine opportunities for self-management.
- The dominant view of leadership is that of the teacher as leader in the classroom.

Demonstrating impact

If they are to be credible, influential and make a difference, then system leaders will need to be comfortable and confident in demonstrating how their activities and proposals will actually make an impact on the system. This implies both an evidence-based approach to their activities and the ability to develop strategies to monitor, review and evaluate, which are implicit to their proposals to influence policy and strategy. Even more fundamental, however, is the ability to generate strategies which are practical and functional.

Leading through trust

Of all the qualities of a system leader, trust is probably the most important. It is difficult to envisage any aspect of their work that is not profoundly dependent on trust – indeed it could be argued that it would be impossible for them to work without trust.

> Leaders should be trustworthy, and this worthiness is an important virtue. Without trust leaders lose credibility. This loss poses difficulties to leaders as they seek to call people to respond to their responsibilities. The painful alternative is to be punitive, seeking to control people through manipulation or coercion. But trust is a virtue in other ways too. The building of trust is an organizational quality. ... Once embedded in the culture of the school, trust works to liberate people to be their best, to give others their best, and to take risks. (Sergiovanni, 2005, page 90)

Bryk and Schneider (2002) distinguish between three types of trust:

- Organic trust is based on the unquestioning acceptance by an individual of the moral and social integrity of a community.
- Contractual trust is based on reciprocity – it is essentially transactional.
- Relational trust is the product of human relationships and interactions – it is characterized by rich networks and high social interdependence.

It will be clear from all that has been written about system leadership that relational trust is the only model that is appropriate to this context. Relational trust is defined by Bryk and Schneider through the following components:

- Respect – recognizing the integrity of all of those involved in a child's education and their mutual interdependence.
- Competence – professional capability and the effective discharge of role and responsibility.
- Personal regard for others – mutual dependence and caring leading to a sense of inter-dependence and reciprocity.
- Integrity – consistency, reliability and a clear sense of moral purpose.

For Bryk and Schneider (2002) 'relational trust constitutes a moral resource for school improvement' (page 34). The power of trust is reinforced by Hargreaves and Fink (2006):

> Trust is a resource. It crates and consolidates energy, commitment, and relation-ships. When trust is broken, people lessen their commitment and withdraw from relationships, and entropy abounds. (pages 213–214)

Leading change and innovation

System leadership in education has to be seen as being fundamentally about change, creativity and innovation. The role itself is symptomatic of change and the under-pinning rationale for system leadership might be seen as securing and consolidating improvement but also, given the context described above, initiating and sustaining transformation, i.e. fundamental and radical change at institutional, local and national level. Thus, system leadership might well be best understood in terms of leadership for change. This topic is discussed in more detail in Chapter 9.

Personal resilience and sustainability

This is the most elusive and complex of the personal qualities. It can be expressed through the '3 Es' –energy, excitement and enthusiasm. There is no book, course or development activity that can build these – they are fundamental to the person. Although they are elusive aspects of leadership they are also the most compelling. System leaders will have to embody hope and optimism as they will often be working in contexts where these qualities are lacking or where the future is unclear or uncertain.

Working as a system leader will be challenging and demanding. It is therefore important that system leaders focus on their own personal sustainability. This means creating time for personal renewal in terms of psychological, physical, social and spiritual well-being:

> The idea of the 'reservoir of hope' is one that has caught the imagination of many. In essence it is about developing personal reserves that can be drawn on in times of need. It is about having enough stored in the reservoir to be able to open the floodgates when needed and then, crucially, being able to replenish the reservoir. What is essential is the time and space to allow a focus on renewal and giving self priority over role. It is also important to develop a personal strategy, which gives form and substance to such reflection. (West-Burnham, 2006)

Behaviours

This section focuses on those behaviours and actions that translate principle into practice. In the final analysis, leadership is about action, while leaders are judged on the basis of their behaviours: how they behave, the appropriateness of their beha-viour and the extent to which their actions make a difference.

As will become clear, the behaviours of system leaders are very much the same as traditional school leaders –what is different is the scope, context and implications of their behaviour.

The following list is not intended to be prescriptive – there are multiple interpretations of leadership behaviour available. Nor is it exhaustive. As system leadership is increasingly understood, so it is imperative that those involved are active participants in learning from that experience, analysing and then codifying it.

Effective system leaders:

- work to build consensus through negotiation and influence
- create, nourish and sustain rich networks that are open and interdependent
- communicate in an appropriate, open and transparent manner, using a range of media with confidence
- model collaborative working by building and developing effective teams
- support the learning and development of others and themselves
- manage time, resources and projects efficiently and effectively
- maintain a clear focus on outcomes and impact
- engage in dialogue to build confidence and understanding
- act as role models, building respect and trust
- work analytically and systematically, using evidence and enquiry based approaches
- support innovation and creativity and model alternative thinking
- work through 'predict and prevent' rather than 'find and fix', i.e. intervention rather than reaction
- recognize, celebrate and consolidate success
- create a working culture based on review and reflection, rigorous monitoring and evaluation
- maintain a focus on *Every Child Matters*, well-being and improving performance.

Building capacity and capability in system leaders:

> If we really want true leaders for the future, and leaders who can become system leaders we need sustainable programmes of training and development ... capacity building and the kind of professional development that helps create leaders or facilitate leadership needs to be part of a plan that's not vulnerable to the availability of funding. (NCSL, 2005a, page 2)

In 2006, NCSL ran a conference on system leadership which investigated the purpose of school leaders leading the system and what was required to ensure that such a role would be productive and achieve its aims. Further outcomes from the conference and other publications from NCSL on system leadership can be found online at www.ncsl.org.uk/publications/publications-systemleadership.cfm#literature

As we have already explained, the drive for system leadership is a relatively new idea. It has almost certainly arisen as a result of schools moving towards greater interdependency and partnership as a result of a number of initiatives from the DCSF, starting with the Excellence in Cities agenda, Excellence Clusters and Education Action Zones. More recently, the *Every Child Matters* agenda and the accompanying extended schools programme has added to a sense of urgency in developing a new form of leadership within the schooling system. The Networked Learning Community programme managed by NCSL and the work being undertaken by the TDA (2007) on remodelling have helped leverage this agenda but, fundamentally, personalization, raising standards and narrowing the achievement gap and the survival of a schooling system are the key drivers behind the system leadership agenda.

In 2007 PricewaterhouseCoopers published its independent study into school leadership; in it system leadership was identified as one of their models of leadership. It went on to recommend:

> DfES should consider how it can stimulate a major ratcheting up of participation in innovative CPD initiatives including at least some of the following elements:
>
> - Secondments into business or the public sector, cross-sectoral mentoring programmes, international exchanges, and study or research opportunities (all of which should be undertaken within a clear set of parameters that focus on outcomes that will have benefits for participants' institutions and/or the wider system);
> - Work-shadowing other school leaders in different contexts;
> - On-going CPD, some of which might be made compulsory, for all sectors of the school workforce, especially those in leadership positions. CPD should include an element of verifiable training in core subjects relating to system-level priorities;
> - Ensuring that school funding includes a sufficient allocation that recognises funding for CPD for leaders; and
> - Tailoring of CPD to sector specific needs, e.g. schools in challenging circumstances, targeting pupils with Special Educational Needs, or effective approaches to collaborative working.
>
> Children's Trusts should be encouraged to develop training that brings together senior leaders from education, health, social services, and other relevant services to provide a joined-up approach and a greater understanding of the ECM agenda. (page 152)

While this recommendation focuses on CPD, for school leadership in general it recognizes the need to build capacity and capability among those working with children and young people, so that we do have the necessary numbers in place to ensure that system leadership from these leaders is indeed a reality. PricewaterhouseCoopers focus on the role of both the DCSF (formerly the DfES) and

Children's Trusts. In reality it is likely to be NCSL and the TDA that develop the wherewithal, through partners, to make this a reality.

The Development Programme for Consultant Leaders is not the only opportunity provided by NCSL to support the development needs of system leaders. Other programmes include the School Improvement Partners' (SIPs) Accreditation Programme and the identification of National Leaders of Education, which:

- provide, with the staff of their schools, additional leadership to schools in difficulty, including those in Ofsted categories and/or schools that may be in transition towards closure, amalgamation, federation or academy status
- advise ministers and other key stakeholders on education policy
- provide advice to NCSL on the development of the National Leaders of Education/National Support School initiative.

It is also worth mentioning the development and learning that took place as a result of Networked Learning Communities, the lessons from which have now been taken on board through the Innovation Unit's Next Practice agenda. What is very clear is the need to develop models of learning and development strategies to support system leaders, as the changes described in this book become embedded in the English education system. System leadership requires a wide range of knowledge, qualities and behaviours that may not necessarily be available as a result of successful headship. System leadership is about attitudinal change as much as anything else. To achieve such a level of learning requires a range of strategies to be in place:

1 The development of a range of cognitive skills: analysis, logic and the interpretation of data.
2 Learning activities that are based on problem solving in real-life situations.
3 Reflection on actual experience based on appropriate feedback.
4 Challenge derived from new ideas, confronting performance, etc.
5 Mentoring and coaching to help mediate the perceived gap between actual and desired performance.
6 A sense of moral purpose, a vocation; a search for personal authenticity.

In practical terms, the most powerful basis for profound learning is supported reflection – support being provided through coaching and mentoring, the use of a reflective journal, structured reading to inform review and, perhaps most importantly, peer review and feedback on actual practice. Perhaps one of the most significant components of such a process is the recognition that learning is a fundamental component of the job itself – not an adjunct or a bonus but a key element in the definition of the role. It is well known that leadership development, especially for headteachers, is the first casualty of any constraint on resources – time or money. This is not to argue for more time to be spent on courses but rather for the principles outlined above to become implicit to personal working patterns, e.g.:

- building review into meetings and all individual and team projects
- scheduling time and space for regular reflection
- establishing a structured and regular pattern of professional reading and creating opportunities to discuss and apply insights gained
- regular meetings with a coach and/or mentor as part of a sustained (and sustaining) developmental relationship
- acting as a coach/mentor to others
- creating networks (virtual and actual) to nourish, support and challenge.

All that has been written so far makes at least one fundamental assumption – that there is the personal motivation and desire to develop as a system leader.

Change – remodelling for personal and organizational change

9

... the reforms have resulted in a revolutionary shift in workforce culture, with clear benefits for many schools. ... teachers' time and work are now focused more directly on teaching and learning. Headteachers and senior managers continue to sustain a heavy workload, but increasingly they are supported by well qualified and experienced managers from outside education which is allowing them to allocate more time for strategic leadership and management. The substantial expansion of the wider workforce at all levels is allowing ... schools to extend the curriculum, provide more care, guidance and support for pupils, and use data more effectively to monitor pupils' progress. (Ofsted, 2007, page 5)

The remodelling agenda

In January 2003, the school workforce unions (except the National Union of Teachers), the Employers' Organization (as the National Employers' Organization for School Teachers (NEOST)), the Welsh Assembly and the DfES (now the DCSF) signed a historic agreement designed to raise standards while at the same time tackling school workforce workload. The agreement was the result of detailed negotiations between the unions, the employers and the government over increasing concerns with regard to growing demands on teacher workload and the underuse of the skills and talents of support staff in schools. In 2001 PricewaterhouseCoopers, in a report for the DfES (PricewaterhouseCoopers, 2001), identified that the majority of teachers were forced, by the nature of their roles, to work longer hours per week than the European Directive on working hours, to which the UK was a signatory, allowed. At the same time, the PricewaterhouseCoopers' report was able to demonstrate that many tasks that teachers were required to undertake did not need the skills of a teacher and would be handled more efficiently by trained support staff. This report formed the basis for the negotiations that followed.

The DfES laid the groundwork for a final agreement in 2002 with the Education Act 2002 and the publication of *Time for Standards: Reforming the Workforce* (DfES, 2002) which set out the future employment vision. While this vision may appear limited by today's requirements, it did provide a commitment to:

- a focus on teaching and learning for teachers, and time to do the job
- a recognition that personalized learning was the way forward, if standards were to be raised and England (and Wales) were to achieve the world-class education levels that the School Effectiveness Unit (SEU) had set as a target as early as 1997
- a commitment to the development of support staff, including new roles and responsibilities
- a commitment to allow headteachers and other school leaders to take on more of a leadership role and a challenge to NCSL to support this.

While system leadership was not particularly highlighted in the document, the development of subsequent programmes, such as the leadership strategy of the London Challenge and the Leadership Incentive Grant (LIG) which followed, can begin to be identified. This book is being written in hindsight and it is always easier to trace histories than predict accurately the future, but DfES expectations at the time are difficult to ignore when the Secretary of State for Education and Skills suggests in the foreword:

> We need a partnership across the whole schools sector so that resources are used to good effect. If we are to give our teachers the help they need, this should involve:
> - More time for high quality, more individualised lesson planning, preparation and pupil assessment;
> - A concerted attack on any bureaucracy that gets in the way of what matters most – teaching and learning and raising standards of pupil achievement;
> - Extra support inside and outside the classroom, with new school support staff filling roles at every level in the school, so that teachers can focus on teaching.
> And we need to help our headteachers, too, including through more time for leadership and through new support from our National College for School Leadership. (DfES, 2002, pages 1–2)

By this time a pathfinder programme was already in place, charged with developing a change management programme that would help schools and subsequently LAs lead effectively the cultural change required. Transforming the Workforce Pathfinder, operating throughout 2002/2003, involved a partnership between the London Leadership Centre at the Institute of Education in London, a small private sector organization, and the 32 schools involved in the pathfinder. The level of success was such that, at least for England, the National Agreement declared 'in England, this programme will be based on that developed as part of the Transforming School Workforce Pathfinder project' (Social Partnership, 2003, page 13). The National Remodelling Team (NRT) was thus born.

At this stage the focus was on teacher workload, but in 2005 extended schools were added to the remit and subsequently Targeted Youth Support. However, it has always been a central claim of the NRT that the change process in use is a generic process and can and should be applied to any major change agenda in a school or local authority.

> Remodelling is a proven approach to managing change that encourages and enables positive and lasting change. It embeds a proactive culture where staff have the skills, experience, confidence and commitment to apply an effective remodelling approach to all significant challenges at all times. (TDA, 2007)

The NRT merged with the Teacher Training Agency (TTA) to form the Training and Development Agency for Schools (TDA) in 2006. The extended remit for this non-departmental public body (NDPB) now included not only teacher recruitment and training and workforce remodelling but also workforce training and development that covered both teachers and the wider workforce working in schools. For the first time, England had in place an agency that was in a position to ensure a targeted focus on school workforce development. A new era had begun.

The remodelling process

The remodelling process involves three aspects. There is the M4D (originally developed by NRT but now owned by TDA) process itself, the associated tools and the particular skills necessary to make it a reality. Remodelling on one level is simple enough to explain but on another level is complex because it not only requires a rational approach to change but also requires a recognition and awareness of both the emotional and political (with a small 'p') enablers and blockers to change that arise if only a rational response is used to leverage a change situation. Good examples abound of failure to win over the hearts and minds of people and instigate the necessary change agenda. A recent case is the Royal Mail strikes in the autumn months of 2007.

The key to remodelling is the TDA's M4D process. Typically, school improvement and development have depended on school leaders: a) identifying the problem; and b) finding a solution. Remodelling argues that, while it may be relatively easy to identify a problem, moving to a solution mode immediately may cause more problems than it actually solves. Such a response was identified in 1990 by Peter Senge (1990) when he suggested:

> The systems viewpoint is generally oriented toward the long-term view. That's why delays and feedback loops are so important. In the short term, you can often ignore them; they're inconsequential. They only come back to haunt you in the long term. (page 92)

The M4D process was developed for schools. It is based on a tried and tested process used since the early 1990s in the private sector. The school change team includes representatives from across the school and should include not only teachers but also representatives from the support staff. Some change teams include governors, parents and pupils.

Although they share many common features, change teams will vary in how they are composed, how often and when they meet, and how they communicate with the rest of the staff, including consultation. This is partly because of the context of the school and partly because of the issues with which the team is dealing. Throughout the process it is essential that all staff and other stakeholders affected by the change are involved. According to the TDA remodelling website:

> Inclusiveness is vital, as people in different roles tend to have different and valuable views and ideas about change. It also enables people to support what they help to create. Broad involvement leads to better and more lasting improvements. It also helps everyone to clearly see and experience the benefits of remodelling. (TDA, 2007)

The process itself contains five clear stages and each stage is important to develop in full.

Mobilise

This is the first stage of the remodelling process. It is during this stage that schools become more aware of the need for change. It is during this time that a change team is formed and the protocols for its existence are agreed. It is also at this stage that the change team needs to understand the process, make sure the members are aware of how to use the tools and begin to develop their understanding of the skills they will need to use throughout the process. By the end of this phase people should:

- understand what is happening and why
- have a good understanding of the issues
- have some understanding of the priorities of the project and potential benefits.

Discover

This stage involves identifying and acknowledging what works well in a school as well as recognizing issues and challenges that the change process should aim to address. This involves working with staff members to discover which elements of school practice are more successful than others and why. It may be important during this stage to identify some 'quick wins' in order to maintain interest and begin to 'win over' some of the doubters. It is also important to realize that during this stage and the next one the enormity of the task will begin to be understood and it is during these stages when the emotions and feelings of all those involved will be at their lowest. This is a natural and well documented reaction to any form of change and it is during this time that the greatest doubts will begin to surface. It is particularly important that school leaders are aware of this and are at their most supportive. At the end of the stage there is a growing awareness of the potential priorities and benefits.

Deepen

During this stage, schools acquire a greater understanding of the scale and scope of the changes that they need to make and the challenges involved. It is also a beneficial time to implement any 'quick wins' identified at the discover stage. These 'quick wins' should help boost morale and promote enthusiasm for the process just at the time when many of the staff are most disillusioned about the whole process. It is also during this stage when car park and corridor conversations are likely to be at their most negative. This is one of the reasons why the team should be aware of what people are thinking, feeling, saying and doing through the whole process of change. At the end of this stage the change team, in particular, should have:

- identified the existing issues or which elements of existing issues that are causing the most challenges
- established the root cause driving these challenges
- further developed an awareness of the potential priorities and benefits.

Develop

At this stage, the change team is in a position to analyse the 'drivers' of the issues that need addressing, and prioritize those that are likely to be able to be resolved while at the same time to have the greatest impact. There are a number of problem-solving techniques within the remodelling toolkit to help the change team to develop made-to-measure, effective and sustainable strategies and solutions to address the highest priority drivers. From here, the team will be able to develop an implementation plan which will enable the school to deliver the solutions. It is during this stage that the emotional curve should begin to show signs of positive recovery, as stakeholders begin to realize that solutions are possible. It is also during this stage that the senior leadership team (SLT) and the governing body will need to be most actively involved in facilitating the change team's progress. If they are seen to block progress, without clear and valid reasons for doing so, it is possible that the motivation of the staff and other stakeholders will quickly decline as a result of this perceived negativity. It is also important for the change team to realize that throughout the process they need to keep both the SLT and the governing body well informed of progress and 'on board'. There is no point in a change team pursuing a solution, no matter how effective it may appear to them, if they later discover there is major opposition to the solution from the SLT. On a more positive note, by the end of this stage:

- the school has a clear picture of the drivers that need to be addressed
- a portfolio of solutions has been selected that addresses the priority issues
- a plan is in place to deliver these solutions.

Deliver

This stage is about implementing the plans that were formed in the develop stage. These will have been initially agreed and a programme put in place for implementation. During this stage, it remains important to ensure that a continuing review process is in place to monitor that the solutions that are put into practice meet the original goals and provide the anticipated benefits identified during earlier stages. It is possible that there may be a need for solutions to be modified to ensure the school moves towards the vision of the future shared by all staff. Monitoring and evaluation are essential for successful delivery. If by this stage things are working well, it is likely that a culture of openness to change and progress enables the school to consistently work to their best, with their staff well supported and confident that their work is valued. Teachers are able to focus on their core teaching work and, consequently, teaching and learning benefits. Schools reach out to share their experiences with other schools and agencies, either directly, face-to-face, or via case studies and articles, such as those on the TDA website (2007). As effective and sustainable solutions are developed by and involve all staff there is enthusiasm and commitment around their implementation and universal support for their success. Staff are confident that this has been a process in which they have been directly involved in managing all aspects of change and, therefore, they have been part of the solution. By the end of this cycle:

- the plan has been agreed and rolled out
- the associated benefits are beginning to be achieved
- a proactive culture of change is now embedded.

It is important to remember, throughout this process, there is a natural emotional curve that will take a dip before the school's motivation picks up.

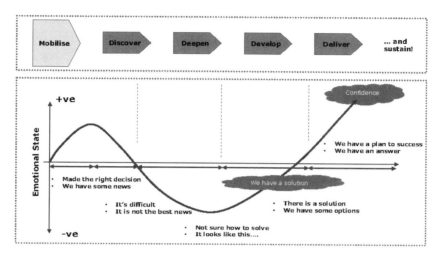

Figure 9.1 The emotional change curve (TDA, 2007)

There are six key aspects to the process on which success depends. These key aspects both legitimize the process and provide it with its uniqueness. More detail on these six aspects is available on the TDA remodelling website (TDA, 2007), but at their basic level they include:

1 Shared leadership
   • A style of leadership that provides a clear direction and focus, drawing on the contributions of all staff and stakeholders.
2 Inclusive culture
   • An enterprising culture that invites all staff to play a part in the change process.
3 Proactive change team
   • An inclusive change team approach to help generate solutions, inform decisions and implement change. It is key to recognize the importance of the inclusion of support staff and how change teams have transformed, in many cases, the ways staff are working together.
4 Broad collaboration
   • Encouraging good practice and collaboration between schools, their stakeholders and associated external agencies.
5 Proven process
   • A proven, structured yet adaptable process for managing change supported by appropriate tools and skills.
6 Rational, political and emotional considerations

- Must include a consideration of the rational, political and emotional dimensions that influence change.

LAs and schools using this process have found that it breaks down barriers and maximizes their resources by harnessing the capability of the whole team. The result is that they have more capacity. They are effectively working smarter not harder.

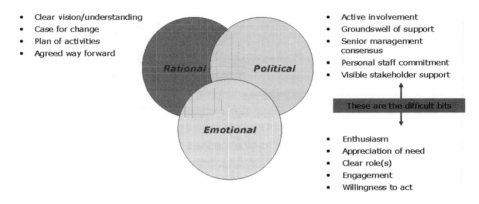

- Clear vision/understanding
- Case for change
- Plan of activities
- Agreed way forward

- Active involvement
- Groundswell of support
- Senior management consensus
- Personal staff commitment
- Visible stakeholder support

These are the difficult bits

- Enthusiasm
- Appreciation of need
- Clear role(s)
- Engagement
- Willingness to act

Figure 9.2 Rational, political and emotional aspects (TDA, 2006)

At this stage we have identified neither the tools provided nor the skills needed to support the process of remodelling. There are a number of tools involved, some already in use in schools and others which may well be less understood. While new tools are being developed and/or introduced from time to time, depending on the programme, a description of the key tools is available online at www.tda.gov.uk/remodelling/managingchange/tools.aspx. Further tools are described in Suzanne Turner's book *Tools for Success: A Manager's Guide* (2003). These tools will need to be adapted for educational use but can still prove valuable. The tools available through the remodelling website and promoted through a variety of programmes have already been transformed for easy use.

The skills involved are straightforward but both necessary and important. They can be acquired but need training and development. They include:

Facilitation: a facilitator helps a team by helping people to voice issues, listen, make decisions and take responsibility. Facilitation is about managing the process of a group to achieve these aims. With a facilitator, teams can overcome any of their own institutionalization. A facilitator helps the team avoid moving into *laissez-faire* solutions. The facilitator's primary role is to manage the process and not to add content.

Coaching: this helps teams/individuals develop and reach beyond themselves. It encourages teams/individuals to own the responsibility for their personal and professional development. It helps teams/individuals find a way to move on from a situation that may be constraining their development or preventing them from attaining an objective.

Feedback: this is a critical aspect of teamwork that helps people to help others to develop and learn. The purpose of feedback is to encourage team members to repeat their positive team behaviours and improve their less helpful ones. Feedback should be seen as a positive and helpful team building tool. Giving and receiving feedback does not come naturally to many – it requires attention and practice.

Dialogue: we bring about change through discussion and conversation. Many of our conversations are replaying long-established patterns of behaviour. Changing our conversations helps us to bring about change. Dialogue is a 'high performance conversation' where we are thinking well together. The challenge in successful dialogue is to balance advocacy ('Let me tell you my reaction to that') with enquiry ('What is your reaction to what I have said?'). Peter Senge describes dialogue as 'the capacity of members of a team to suspend assumptions and enter into a genuine "thinking together" ' (1990, page 10).

The importance of the remodelling process should not be underrated by a system leader. There are three fundamental reasons for this. First, it is the supported approach to change adopted by the Department and the TDA and has worked with the implementation of the National Agreement, extended services in schools and Targeted Youth Support, which involves multi-agency working. Second, it is a generic process that can be applied to any change scenario. It builds on the best insights for change in the private sector as well as incorporating thinking from the public sector. The aim of the process is to bring about change by drawing on the best available theory and adapting this theory to make it work at a practical level. Third, many schools will already have adopted this approach and be using it as a natural way of driving forward their own change agenda. Not every school headteacher has adopted it with uncritical enthusiasm but there is equally evidence to suggest that where they have not adopted this approach there is a minimal amount of workforce modernization or change taking place.

For example, the recent Ofsted report into workforce reform and implementation of the National Agreement, referenced at the start of this chapter, points out:

> Little attention was paid to linking workforce reform to wider school improvement initiatives or guidance given on prioritising national agendas. The need to monitor the impact of actions on standards was rarely considered. This was partly because the majority of local authorities were still establishing the procedures and systems they needed to support their schools. (Ofsted, 2007, page 8)

School improvement planning

In order to help schools link extended services with their traditional core business, teaching and learning, and measure impact, the TDA has developed a School Improvement Planning Framework based on the remodelling process in partnership with 150 schools and various other organizations. The framework does not set out to provide a new format for school improvement planning. The TDA believes that schools already know what they are doing in this field. Instead it has co-created a framework designed to help schools link the standards agenda and their extended services into one coherent plan. It enables schools to ensure they take account of everything that is going on in the school and to measure the impact this may be having on pupil achievement.

According to the TDA, what makes the school improvement planning framework different is:

- the tools are accessible, adaptable and can be easily built into existing school improvement activities
- schools can tailor the tools to fit their own circumstances
- the tools make it possible to engage staff, parents, pupils and the wider community in a meaningful way from the outset
- it enables schools to monitor and measure the impact of their planning activities on pupils.

The framework consists of eight modules incorporating 35 supporting tools and exercises.

1 **Prepare and engage.** This module focuses on understanding who to involve (within and beyond the school) and how to engage them. It is designed to help with the development of a shared vision of goals for the school and clarifying what it is the school wants to achieve.

2 **Identify objectives.** This section consists of three modules designed to help develop balanced and evidence-based objectives within and beyond the classroom.

2a **Teaching and curriculum.** This module helps the school to create key objectives in the curriculum, the classroom and beyond the classroom using data to generate learning objectives. It also helps the gathering of input from key stakeholders to enrich the understanding of what supports learning in the classroom.

2b **Learning potential.** This module helps with exploring the key characteristics of successful learners. The use of it aims to help the school understand how the performance of pupils can be influenced through using what happens outside the formal learning environment.

2c **ECM outcomes.** The third module in Section 2 examines the role of the school in influencing ECM outcomes in a way that reflects the school and community context and builds upon local authority plans.

3 **Develop and prioritize solutions.** This helps schools to decide how to ensure the school's objectives deliver impact within and outside the classroom. It uses different approaches to identify appropriate solutions to meet the school's objectives. It is particularly useful when the school is involving the support of external parties.

4 **Deliver.** This module leads schools through the implementation of the plan. This is achieved through assigning responsibilities, allocating resources, agreeing deadlines and monitoring progress.

5 **Personalization.** Personalized learning is a key methodology for developing the talents of all pupils. This module helps develop this process through encouraging conversations that can lead to a better understanding of the broader needs of individual pupils. Consistent with the aim of the framework it also encourages schools to identify ways in which these needs can be influenced by extended services.

6 **Demonstrate impact.** The final module helps schools to develop ways in which the information generated can be used to demonstrate and monitor the impact of extended services on children and young people.

Further detail on the School Improvement Planning Framework is available online at www.tda.gov.uk/schoolimprovement

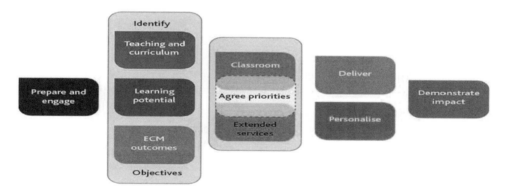

Figure 9.3 The School Improvement Planning Framework (TDA, 2007)

For system leaders who are working directly with schools, for example as a school improvement partner, executive headteacher or consultant, this framework is a useful tool. It is flexible rather than prescriptive, and the tools can be selected by the school to suit its need and context. How it develops in a school is a matter for the school itself; there are no imposed commitments. In many of the schools, where it was developed, it was assimilated into existing practice.

Conclusion

Throughout this book we have tried to explain briefly what we believe system leadership actually is and how it can be used to help develop a better understanding in schools of what a world-class education system might mean. Neither of us claim to be experts in this field but we do believe it is important to make things as simple as possible but no simpler. It is no longer a reality to continue to live in the educational world that served the industrial era so well. Those days have long gone. Nor is it possible for schools to continue to exist in glorious isolation. The 'secret garden' began to vanish in the mid 1980s; the notion that the teacher was the sole person in charge has been under scrutiny since the late 1990s. Ideas around collaboration, partnership and multi-agency working are not in themselves new but the principles of trust and shared leadership in such relationships are. System leadership becomes a necessary phenomenon in such a context. We trust that the ideas in this book may help the further development of system leadership as it begins to become embedded as a way of working.

We wish to finish the book with a quote from the futurologist John Schaar, which Pat Collarbone always uses to finish her presentations. We do not know the date except we think it was in the early 1960s. But it summarizes well the agenda now faced by schools in England, and therefore the purpose of system leadership:

> The future is not a result of choices among alternative paths offered by the present, but a place that is created – created first in the mind and will, created next in activity.
>
> The future is not some place we are going to, but one we are creating. The paths are not to be found, but made, and the activity of making them, changes both the maker and the destination.

References

Audit Commission (2006) *More than the Sum*, London: Audit Commission

Balakrishnan, A. (2006) 'Unexpected fall in output spells trouble for industrial recovery', *The Guardian*, 8 August

Ballantyne, P., Jackson, D., Temperley, J., Jopling, M. with Lieberman, J. (2006) *System Leadership in Action*, Nottingham: NCSL

Berry, N. (2007) 'On being a SIP and being Sipped', *Secondary Headship*, 58(October): 1–8

Bohm, D. (1996) *On Dialogue*, London: Routledge

Bond, K., Farrar, M., West-Burnham, J. and Otero, G. (2006) 'Leading beyond boundaries: *Every Child Matters* and system leadership within communities', in Carter, K. and Sharpe, T. (eds), *School Leaders Leading the System: System Leadership in Perspective*, Nottingham: NCSL

Bryk, A. and Schneider, B. (2002) *Trust in Schools*, New York: Russell Sage Foundation

Centre for Longitudinal Studies (2007) Institute of Education, University of London www.cls.ioe.ac.uk/

Collarbone, P. (2007) *Care Matters: Best Practice in Schools Working Group Report*, Nottingham: DfES Publications

Dantley, M.E. and Tillman, L.C. (2006) *Social Justice and Moral Transformative Leadership*, in Marshall, C. and Oliva, M (eds), *Leadership for Social Justice*, Boston, Mass.: Pearson Education

Department for Children, Schools and Families (2005) *What are Federations?*, www.standards.dfes.gov.uk/federations/what_are_federations/?version=1

Department for Children, Schools and Families (DCSF) (2007a) *The Standards Site*, www.standards.dfes.gov.uk/primary/publications/foundation_stage/eyfs/

Department for Children, Schools and Families (DCSF) (2007b) *A New Relationship with Schools: The School Improvement Partner's Brief Edition 3*, London: DCSF

Department for Education and Employment (DfEE) (1998) *Teachers Meeting the Challenge of Change*, London: Stationery Office

Department for Education and Employment (DfEE) (2001) *Schools: Building on Success*, London: Stationery Office

Department for Education and Skills (DfES) (2002) *Time for Standards: Reforming the Workforce*, Nottingham: DfES Publications

Department for Education and Skills (DfES) (2003) *Excellence and Enjoyment: A Strategy for Primary Schools*, Nottingham: DfES Publications

Department for Education and Skills (DfES) (2004a) *Every Child Matters: Next Steps*, Nottingham: DfES Publications

Department for Education and Skills (DfES) (2004b) *Every Child Matters: Change for Children*, Nottingham: DfES Publications

Department for Education and Skills (DfES) (2004c) *Five Year Strategy for Children and Learners*, Nottingham: DfES Publications.

Department for Education and Skills (DfES) (2005a) *Youth Matters*, London: Stationery Office

Department for Education and Skills (DfES) (2005b) Prospectus sets out how schools will offer more services in their communities, Press Release, 13 June.

Department for Education and Skills (DfES) (2005c) *Extended Schools: Access to Opportunities and Services for All: A Prospectus*, Nottingham: DfES Publications

Department for Education and Skills (DfES) (2005d) *National Framework for Mentoring and Coaching*, London: DfES

Department for Education and Skills (DfES) (2006) *Youth Matters: Next Steps*, Nottingham: DfES Publications

Department for Education and Skills (DfES) (2007) *Care Matters: Time for Change*, London: Stationery Office

Department for Education and Skills (DfES)/Ofsted (2004) *A New Relationship with Schools*, London: HMSO

Desforges, C. (2003) *The Impact of Parental Involvement, Parental Support and Family Education on Pupil Achievements and Adjustment: A Literature Review*, London: DfES Research Report RR433

Diamond, J. (2005) *Collapse*, London: Allen Lane

Drucker, P. (1969) *The Age of Discontinuity: Guidelines to our Changing Society*, Oxford: Butterworth-Heinemann

Duignan, P. (2006) *Educational Leadership Key Challenges and Ethical Tensions*, Cambridge: Cambridge University Press

Earl, L., Katz, S., Elgie, S., Jaafar, S.B. and Foster, L. (2006) *How Networked Learning Communities Work*, Toronto: Aporia Consulting

Every Child Matters (2007) www.everychildmatters.gov.uk/

Fullan, M. (2003) *The Moral Imperative of School Leadership*, Thousand Oaks, Calif.: Corwin Press

Fullan, M. (2004) *Systems Thinkers in Action: Moving beyond the Standards Plateau*, Nottingham: DfES Publications

Fullan, M. (2005) *Leadership and Sustainability*, Thousand Oaks, Calif.: Corwin Press

Gardner, H. (2004) *Changing Minds*, Boston, Mass.: Harvard Business School Press

Gladwell, M. (2000) *The Tipping Point*, London: Abacus

Goddard Park (2007) www.goddardpark-pri.swindon.sch.uk/

Goleman, D. (2006) *Social Intelligence*, London: Hutchinson

Goleman, D., Boyatzis, R. and McKee, A. (2002) *The New Leaders: Transforming the Art of Leadership into the Science of Results*, London: Little, Brown

Handy, C. (1989) *The Age of Unreason*, London: Hutchinson

Hargreaves, A. (2003) *Education Epidemic: Transforming Secondary Schools through Iinnovation Networks*, London: Demos

Hargreaves, A. and Fink, D. (2006) *Sustainable Leadership*, San Francisco, Calif.: John Wiley & Sons

Harris, A., Allen, T. and Goodall, J. (2007) 'Understanding the Reasons why Schools do or do not Fully Engage with the ECM/ES Agenda', Warwick: University of Warwick (unpublished)

Havel, V. (1994) Speech in Philadelphia, Pa, June

Heppell, S. (2007) *Power to the People's Pockets*, Stephen Heppell's Weblog, www.heppell.net/

Her Majesty's Chief Inspector of Education, Children's Services and Skills (2007), *Annual Report*, London: Ofsted, www.ofsted.gov.uk/publications/annualreport 0607

HM Treasury (2003) *Every Child Matters: Change for Children*, London: Stationery Office

HM Treasury, DfES, DWP and DTI (2004) *Choice for Parents, the Best Start for Children: A Ten Year Strategy for Childcare*, London: Stationery Office

Hobson, A. (2003) *Review of Literature on Coaching/Mentoring New Headteachers*, www.ncsl.org.uk/mediastore/image2/hobson-mentoring-and-coaching-full.pdf

Hock, D. (1999) *Birth of the Chaordic Age*, San Francisco, Calif.: Berrett-Koehler Publishers

Hopkins, D. (2005) A short primer on systems leadership, presentation at the Institute of Education, University of London, 26 September

Horley Learning Partnership (HLP) (2007) www.horleylp.org.uk/

Houses of Parliament (1988) Education Reform Act, London: Stationery Office

Houses of Parliament (1998) Standards and Framework Act, London: Stationery Office

Houses of Parliament (2002) Education Act 2002, London: Stationery Office

Houses of Parliament (2004) The Children Act 2004, London: Stationery Office

Houses of Parliament (2005) Education Act 2005, London: Stationery Office

Houses of Parliament (2006) Education and Inspections Act 2006, London: Stationery Office

Houston, P.D. (2004) *Advancing System Leadership*, www.aasa.org/publications/ saarticledetail.cfm?ItemNumber=1106

Innovation Unit, NCSL and Demos (2007) *System Leadership and Governance: Leadership Beyond Institutional Boundaries*, Nottingham: NCSL

Laming, H. (2003) *The Victoria Climbié Inquiry Report*, London: Stationery Office

Leithwood, K., Day, C., Sammons, P., Harris, A. and Hopkins, D. (2007) *Seven Strong Claims about Successful School Leadership*, Nottingham: NCSL

Lindsay, G., Arweck, E., Chapman, C., Goodall, J., Muijs, D. and Harris, A. (2005) *Evaluation of the Federations Programme 2nd Interim Report*, Warwick: University of Warwick

Marx, K. (1867) *Das Kapital*, reprinted 2002, Boston, Mass.: Adamant Media Corporation

Microsoft (2007) ICT at the heart of learning, www.microsoft.com/uk/education/heartoflearning.mspx

Morrison, K. (2002) *School Leadership and Complexity Theory*, London: RoutledgeFalmer

National College for School Leadership (NCSL) (2005) *Executive Headship: A Study of Heads who are Leading Two or More Secondary or Special Schools*, Nottingham: NCSL

National College for School Leadership (NCSL) (2006) *Learning About Learning Networks*, Nottingham: NCSL

National College for School Leadership (NCSL) (2007) *A Guide for National Leaders of Education, National Support Schools, Local Authorities and Client School Leaders*, Nottingham: NCSL

North Prospect (2007) www.northprospect.plymouth.sch.uk/

Office for Standards in Education (Ofsted) (2006) *Extended Services in Schools and Children's Centres*, London: Ofsted Publications

Office for Standards in Education (Ofsted) (2007) *Reforming and Developing the School Workforce*, London: Ofsted Publications

O'Leary, D. and Craig, J. (2007) *System Leadership Lessons from the Literature*, Nottingham: DEMOS and NCSL

Papert, S. and Caperton, G. (1999) *Vision for Education: The Caperton–Papert Platform*, paper prepared for the National Governors' Association, St Louis, Miss., August

Perkins, D. (2003) *King Arthur's Round Table*, Hoboken, NJ.: John Wiley & Sons

PricewaterhouseCoopers (2001) *Teacher Workload Study*, London: DfES

PricewaterhouseCoopers (2007) *Independent Study into School Leadership* RB818, London: DfES

Putnam, R. (2000) *Bowling Alone*, New York: Simon and Schuster

Schwarz, R. (2002) *The Skilled Facilitator*, San Francisco, Calif.: Jossey-Bass

Senge, P. (1990) *The Fifth Discipline*, New York: Doubleday

Senge, P., Cambron McCabe, N., Lucas, T., Smith, B., Dutton, J. and Kleiner, A. (2000) *Schools that Learn*, New York: Doubleday

Sergiovanni, T. (2005) *Strengthening the Heartbeat*, San Francisco, Calif.: Jossey-Bass

Silins, H. and Mulford, B. (2002) *Leadership and School Results*, in Leithwood, K. and Hallinger, P. (eds), *Second International Handbook of Educational Leadership and Administration*, Norwell, Mass.: Kluwer Academic Press

Social Partnership (2003) *Raising Standards and Tackling Workload: A National Agreement*, Nottingham: DfES, www.tda.gov.uk/upload/resources/pdf/n/na_standards_workload.pdf

Staffordshire Children's Trust (2007) www.staffordshirechildrenstrust.org.uk/clp/

Tapscott, D. and Williams, A.D. (2006) *Wikinomics: How Mass Collaboration Changes Everything*, New York: Penguin Books

Training and Development Agency (TDA) (2007) http://tda.gov.uk/remodelling.aspx

Turner, S. (2003) *Tools for Success: A Manager's Guide*, Maidenhead: McGraw Hill Professional

UNICEF (2007) Child poverty in perspective: an overview of child well-being in rich countries, Innocenti Report Card 7, Florence: UNICEF, www.unicef.org/irc

Wenger, E. (1998) *Communities of Practice*, Cambridge: Cambridge University Press

West-Burnham, J. (2006) *Hope Springs Eternal*, NCSL: *ldr* online magazine, March, www.ldr-magazine.co.uk/

West-Burnham, J., Farrar, M. and Otero, G. (2007) *Schools and Communities*, London: Network Continuum

Wigan Community (2007) www.wigan.gov.uk/Services/EducationLearning/Schools/ExtendedHours/

Worldmapper (2007) www.worldmapper.org/index.html

Zohar, D. (1997) *Reviving the Corporate Brain*, San Francisco, Calif.: Berrett-Koehler

Index

ability 74
academic theory 13
Academies 9
accountability 16, 22, 24, 25, 34, 44, 49, 58, 62, 64, 82, 89
adult learning 11
after school activities 38
Asia 2
aspiration 74
assistant heads 18
attainment 71
Audit Commission 21, 71, 72, 73, 74, 77
Australia 2
authority 82, 90
autonomy 16, 61

basic skills 74
beacon schools 9
behaviour support 32
behaviours 92–6
best practice 85
Blair, Tony 27
breakfast clubs 38
Building Schools for the Future 5

CAF see Common Assessment Framework
CAMHS see child and adolescent mental health services
capital programmes 1
Care Matters: Time for Change 33
career development 18
central government 22
Centre for Longitudinal Studies 9
change teams 100, 103
child and adolescent mental health services (CAMHS) 32
child poverty 72

childcare 27, 28, 29, 31, 37
  provision 43
Children Act 2004 21, 28, 29
Children and Young People's Plan 29, 40
children in care 33–4
children's centres 31, 43, 80
children's commissioner 29
children's health 80
Children's Trusts 28, 94, 95
China 2
  economic growth 70
Church of England 3
City Learning Centres 9
civic community 76
civic engagement 77
class 2, 80
Climbié, Victoria 26, 29
CLPs see community and learning partnerships
cluster managers 45
clusters 19, 20, 61, 64, 65–6, 67, 68, 69, 70, 83
coaches 56, 57, 96
coaching 49, 58–9, 95, 104–5
coalitions 88
cognitive skills 95
collaboration 61, 103, 108
Common Assessment Framework (CAF) 32
communication 83, 89
communism, collapse of 70
communities of practice 89
community 75–81
community and learning partnerships (CLPs) 44
community initiatives 20–1
community renewal projects 21
competence 91

competition 69
comprehensive schools 2
consensus 93
consultancy 49, 57–8
consultant leaders 51
consultants 56, 57
consultation 21
continual professional development (CPD) 65, 67, 94
CPD *see* continual professional development
curriculum 5, 14–19, 37, 65, 74, 80, 106 *see also* National Curriculum
  Foundation Stage 30

DCSF *see* Department for Children, Schools and Families
Demos 17
Department for Children, Schools and Families (DCSF) 8, 94, 97 *see also* Department for Education and Skills
Department for Education and Skills (DfES) 7, 8, 11, 14, 66, 94, 97, 98 *see also* Department for Children, Schools and Families
  Innovations Unit 83
dependency 14
dependency culture 53
deprivation 8, 71
deputy heads 18
Development Programme for Consultant Leaders 95
DfES *see* Department for Education and Skills
disability 8, 33, 73, 80
distributed leadership 19
Drucker, Peter 3
dysfunctional family structures 33

Early Years 29–31
Early Years Foundation Stage (EYFS) 30
Early Years Framework 8
ECM *see* Every Child Matters
economic development 8

Education Act 1944 2
Education Act 2002 7, 38, 39, 66, 98
Education Act 2005 7
Education Action Zones 94
education acts 7
Education and Inspections Act 2006 7
Education Reform Act 1988 8
education system 25, 62
Education Village, Darlington 67
educational leaders 73
educational research 85
EiC *see* Excellence in Cities
elementary education 2
employers 65
Employers' Organization 97
employment opportunities 81
environmental issues 80
equity 8–9, 14, 87
ES *see* extended schools
ESCOs *see* extended school coordinators
ethnic minorities 73
ethnicity 8
evaluation 102
Every Child Matters (ECM) 9–11, 21, 26–36, 46, 47, 67, 74, 75, 79, 87, 93, 94
Every Child Matters: Change for Children 28, 37
Every Child Matters: Next Steps 28
evidence-based assessment 52
executive leadership 20
excellence 14, 87
Excellence and Enjoyment: A Strategy for Primary Schools 7
Excellence Clusters 9, 94
Excellence in Cities (EiC) 9, 94
  action zones 9
executive headship 53–4
expertise 86
extended school coordinators (ESCOs) 41
extended schools (ES) 35, 37, 40–4, 45–8
EYFS *see* Early Years Foundation Stage

facilitation 49, 59–60

facilitators 56, 57, 104
faith schools 65
family support 27, 28, 29
FE *see* further education
federalism 65–6
federations 19, 20, 61, 66–7, 68, 69, 70, 83
    hard 66, 67
    soft 66
Five Year Strategy 14
foster parents 34
Foundation Stage
    curriculum 30
    Early Learning Goals 72
14–19 curriculum 65
free school meals 8
FSEEs *see* Full Service Extended Schools
Full Service Extended Schools (FSEEs) 10,
    38
further education (FE) 38
    colleges 65

Gemeinschaft 76
gender 8, 73, 80
Gesellschaft 76
governing bodies 41, 42, 43, 44, 45, 102
government 97
governors 42
grammar schools 2
Greenland 77
Gutenberg, Johannes 3

headship 22, 79, 82
headteacher conferences 49
headteachers 6, 15, 16, 18, 21, 23, 41, 42, 43,
    45, 46, 47, 51, 52, 54, 71, 78, 80, 90, 95,
    97, 105
helpers 57
Heppell, Stephen 4
HLP *see* Horley Learning Partnership
Horley Learning Partnership (HLP) 40

inclusion 87
inclusiveness 100

independence 61
India 2
    economic growth 70
industrial revolution 1–3
information services 3
information technologies 3
innovation 85
Innovation Unit 17
    Next Practice agenda 95
inspections 8
Institute of Education, London 9, 98
institutional autonomy 69
integrity 91
intelligence 74
interdependence 14, 61, 70, 77, 91, 94
internet 4, 70
interpersonal strategies 88
isolationalism 16

Kelly, Ruth 10
Key Stage 3 8
knowledge 3, 85, 86, 89

Labour party 6
Laming Inquiry 26–7
Laming, Lord 26–7
LAs *see* local authorities
leadership 14
Leadership Incentive Grant (LIG) 9, 98
league tables 16
learning 4, 5, 47, 62, 63, 74, 76, 77, 95,
    106
    personalized 1
learning activities 95
Learning and Skills Council 65
LEAs see local education authorities 2
legislation 2
life chances 73–5
LIG *see* Leadership Incentive Grant
literacy 8, 74
local authorities (LAs) 21, 29, 41, 43, 45, 53,
    65, 98, 104
local education authorities (LEAs) 2

Local Safeguarding Children Boards 29
London Challenge 33, 98
London Leadership Centre 98
London, bombings of 7 July 8
lunchtime activities 38

M4D process 99, 100
maintained schools 48
market economy 16
Marx, Karl
 Das Kapital 3
mass media 3
maths 8
mental health 28
mentoring 49, 58–9, 95
  schemes 50
mentors 56, 57, 96
meta learning 63
Millennium Cohort Study 9
monitoring 102
moral purpose 87
More than the Sun 71
motivation 74, 103
multi-agency working 108
multi-tasking 5
Muslim community 8
mutuality 61

National Agreement 105
National College for School Leadership
  (NCSL) 17, 33, 35, 45, 46, 51, 54, 55,
  62, 63, 83, 94, 95, 98
  conference 93
National Curriculum 8, 30, 72 *see also*
  curriculum
National Employers' Organization for School
  Teachers (NEOST) 97
National Framework for Mentoring and
  Coaching 58–9
national leaders of education (NLE) 54–5
National Literacy and Numeracy Strategies 6,
  8, 15
National Remodelling Team (NRT) 99

National Standards for Headteachers 46, 79,
  83
National Support School initiative 95
National Union of Teachers 97
NCSL *see* National College for School
  Leadership
negotiators 59
NEOST see National Employers'
  Organization for School Teachers
Networked Learning Communities 62, 63,
  65, 69, 94, 95
  projects 63
networking 83
networks 19, 20, 61, 62–4, 67, 68, 69, 70, 83,
  88, 93, 96
New Relationship with Schools, A 7
New York, bombings of 9/11 8
NLE *see* national leaders of education
non-linear problem solving 5
North America 2
NRT *see* National Remodelling Team
NSCL Networked Learning Communities 68
numeracy 74

Ofsted 7, 8, 34, 46, 66, 95, 105
organization theory 13
outcomes 93

Papert, Seymour 4
Parent Councils 79
parental choice 16
parenting 10–11, 27
parenting support 38
partner schools 53
partnership 108
PAYP *see* positive activities for young people
PCTs *see* primary care trusts
performance tables 8
personal resilience 92
personalization 5
personalized learning 1
police 39
policy development 85

policy-makers 1
politics 81
positive activities for young people (PAYP) 32
poverty 72, 73
pregnancy 29
PricewaterhouseCoopers 11, 17, 82, 94, 97
primary care trusts (PCTs) 39
primary schools 38, 65
printing press 3
private schools 2
professional helping strategies 55
professionalism 52
promotion 18
public sector 11
public services 37
pupil achievement 106
pupil progress and attainments 51

race 8, 73, 80
Raising Standards and Tackling Workload: A National Agreement 41
reciprocity 91
reflection 95
remodelling 99–105
research and development 3
residential homes 34
respect 91

School Effectiveness Unit (SEU) 98
school improvement and development 72, 99
   planning 106–8
   policies 69
school improvement and standards agenda 51
School Improvement Partners (SIPs) 50, 51–2
   Accreditation Programme 95
School Improvement Planning Framework 107
school leaders 1, 6, 11–12, 19, 75, 78
school leadership 22
school leaving age 2
school management 17

school renewal 72
school workforce unions 97
schools 65, 75–8
   beacon 9
   comprehensive 2
   design 5
   faith 65
   grammar 2
   maintained 48
   primary 38, 65
   private 2
   secondary 10, 38
   secondary modern 2
   self-managing 8
   special 65
Schools Building on Success 6
Schopenhauer 67
science 8
secondary modern schools 2
secondary schooling 2
secondary schools 10, 38
Secretary of State for Education and Skills 98
SEF *see* self-evaluation form
self-assessment 51
self-evaluation form (SEF) 40
self-management 51, 90
self-managing schools 8
Senge, Peter 13
senior leadership teams (SLTs) 45, 102
SEU *see* School Effectiveness Unit
shared leadership 19
shared learning 89
SIPs *see* school improvement partners
SLTs *see* senior leadership teams
social capital 73, 75–8
social class 73
social engagement 88
social entrepreneurship 80
social inclusion 8
social justice 87
social needs
   children 87
social networks 77

social relationships 88
social services 27, 28, 39
social workers 45
software 69
special education 80
special educational needs 94
special needs staff 45
special schools 65
specialist schools 9
stakeholders 100, 102, 106
standards 6, 8, 97, 106
Standards and Framework Act 1998 8
Standards Fund 41
state system 16
storytelling 86
student voice 63
Sunday school system 2
super learning days 63
support staff 97, 98
Sure Start funding 43
systems theory 13

Targeted Youth Support 99, 105
TDA *see* Training and Development Agency
    for Schools
teacher recruitment 99
teacher training 99
Teacher Training Agency (TTA) 99
teachers 5, 12, 97, 102
Teachers Meeting the Challenge of Change 6
teaching 47, 63, 106
technology 5
Time for Standards: Reforming the Workforce
    98
timetables 87

Training and Development Agency for Schools
    (TDA) 35, 46, 94, 95, 99, 105
    remodelling website 100, 102, 103
    School Improvement Planning Programme
       106
Transforming the Workforce Pathfinder
    project 98–9
transparency 52
trust 90–1, 93
    relational 91
TTA *see* Teacher Training Agency

underachievement 71, 72
UNICEF 72
unions 97

voluntary committees 44
voluntary services 31
volunteering 77

Warwick, University of 35, 46, 47
websites 4
Welsh Assembly 97
Wikinomics 69–70
workforce 1
working class 2
workload 97
workshops 63

Young People's Parliament 33
Youth Matters 31–3
youth offending teams 39
youth organizations 39
youth support 32
youth workers 45